The Racial
Wealth Gap

NORTON
SHORTS

The Racial Wealth Gap

A Brief History

MEHRSA BARADARAN

W. W. NORTON & COMPANY
Independent Publishers Since 1923

To my daughters Cyra, Lucia, and Ramona

For information about permission to reproduce selections from
this book, write to Permissions, W. W. Norton & Company, Inc.,
500 Fifth Avenue, New York, NY 10110

For information about special discounts for bulk purchases, please contact
W. W. Norton Special Sales at specialsales@wwnorton.com or 800-233-4830

Manufacturing by Lakeside Book Company
Production manager: Delaney Adams

ISBN: 978-0-393-88182-0

W. W. Norton & Company, Inc.
500 Fifth Avenue, New York, NY 10110
www.wwnorton.com

W. W. Norton & Company Ltd.
15 Carlisle Street, London W1D 3BS

Authorized EU representative:
EAS, Mustamäe tee 50, 10621 Tallinn, Estonia

10 9 8 7 6 5 4 3 2 1

History is not the past. It is the present. We carry our history with us. We are our history. If we pretend otherwise, we are literally criminals. I attest to this: the world is not white; it never was white, cannot be white. White is a metaphor for power, and that is simply a way of describing Chase Manhattan Bank.

—James Baldwin

1860
(Civil War Era)

White families hold *60x* the wealth of Black families.

1880
(End of Reconstruction)

White families hold *20x* the wealth of Black families.

White-Black Wealth Gap
1900–Present

Ratio of white per capita wealth to Black per capita wealth

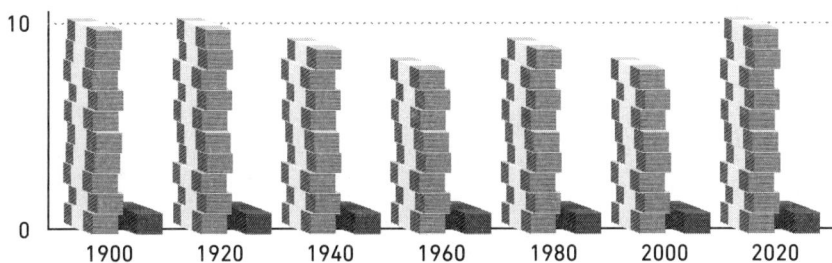

Since 1900, white families have held approximately *10x* the wealth of Black families.

This book explains why the gap has never narrowed.

CONTENTS

Introduction

What is the racial wealth gap? The phrase describes a statistical reality: when we track differences in wealth among racial groups, we discover that whites hold a disproportionate amount of wealth compared to Black, Indigenous, and other groups of non-white Americans.* This book will provide a condensed overview of the key programs and policies that helped shape that modern landscape of racial inequality, outlining how such a gap was created and maintained and how it will continue to grow if not addressed. But *The Racial Wealth Gap* is not just about how discrimination, exclusion, and exploitation created economic disparities linked to race. It is about how powerful insiders

---

* While this book is focused on the Black-white racial wealth gap, it is with full recognition that the same historic harms that have been perpetrated on the Black community have also been perpetrated on other communities, especially the Indigenous populations whose genocide was a precursor to the slave plantation economy. More has been and can be written about how each of these historic crimes affected other dispossessed and oppressed populations and the ideologies and legal machineries that enabled them. It is my hope that understanding the particulars that led to the Black-white racial wealth gap can shed light on these other historic tragedies.

siphoned off more than their share of the nation's wealth using race and racism as a political weapon. Indeed, as this book goes to press, the world's richest man, Elon Musk, whose fortune was made possible by government subsidies, has taken control of the federal government, promising to eliminate DEI and woke ideology.

Just a few years prior, America did seem to be on the cusp of a racial reckoning. On May 25, 2020, as the COVID pandemic raged and Donald Trump was nearing the end of his first term in office, George Floyd was murdered by police officer Derek Chauvin. It is unclear why this particular murder of a Black man by a police officer sparked a worldwide Black Lives Matter uprising, but it is undeniable that Floyd's death and the subsequent protest movement led to a nationwide racial reckoning unlike anything the country had experienced in recent history. Suddenly, Americans were reading about systemic racism, the failure of Reconstruction, the landing of the first slave ships in 1619, Jim Crow, redlining, and the racial wealth gap. Indeed, all of this history was relevant to understanding Floyd's murder.

By the end of 2020, the racial-discrimination protests that had begun five years earlier had spread across the world—to Europe, Asia, Africa, South America, and the Middle East, with protesters from Paris to Tehran holding up pictures of George Floyd and signs declaring, "Black Lives Matter," "Say His Name," and "No Justice, No Peace." Such worldwide unrest summoned for many memories of the global revolutions and domestic race riots of 1967 and 1968, which occurred during the Lyndon B. Johnson administration. In an effort to understand the cause of the conflict, Johnson initiated the National Advisory Commission on Civil Disorders, also known as the Kerner Commission. This commission launched an extensive study, conducted by hundreds of social scientists and researchers, and ultimately concluded that the riots sprang from a long-fermenting stew of racism, inequity, discrimination, and poverty. The report noted that the most salient factor, though, was segregation: "Segregation and poverty have created in the racial ghetto a destructive environment totally unknown to most white Americans. What white Americans have never fully understood—but what the Negro can never forget—is that white society is deeply implicated in the ghetto. White institutions created it, white institutions maintain it, and white society condones it."

The Kerner Commission's report was a stark and scathing critique of white indifference to the Black American condition. It sounded an alarm bell, too, claiming that "our Nation is moving toward two societies, one black, one white—separate and unequal." The commission advocated for swift, thorough government intervention in the form of integration and wealth-building programs specifically designed to assist the country's struggling Black population.

Since the Kerner Commission made its report, the American government has declined to take public responsibility for the ills leveled at Black Americans, past or present. No programs that bear any resemblance to the ones recommended by the report have been attempted in earnest. Shortly after the report's release, President Johnson announced that he would not be pursuing another term in office. Less than a week later, Martin Luther King Jr. was assassinated in Memphis, and the politically savvy Richard Nixon leveraged the country's racial disquiet into a campaign fraught with anti-Black dog whistles that won him the presidency.

The transformations America underwent over the course of Nixon's presidency are evident to this day, and the racial wealth gap remains a gaping wound in the economic landscape. It is no wonder, in light of these circumstances, that Americans are still protesting for Black lives.

It is also unsurprising that as soon as the worldwide Black Lives Matter protests surged, a backlash and retrenchment began—although not before the protests fundamentally changed American politics, culture, and even corporate structures. In 2020, there was hardly a corporation, university, or government office that did not begin diversity, equity, and inclusion (DEI) initiatives and racial education programs or renew its dedication to existing policies. Having released a book about racism in banking in 2017, I found myself speaking to groups of employees at places like Netflix, Apple, and Amazon about topics such as the Reconstruction-era Freedman's Savings Bank. This created a strange feeling of whiplash. I had written the book during the Obama era, a Cassandra shouting into the void that this gap was a massive societal failure despite apparent signs of racial progress. Now I was being welcomed into JPMorgan Chase and asked to explain how the mainstream banking system had perpetually blocked Black wealth accumulation to feed its own coffers. Even more discomforting was the fact that it took George Floyd's horrific death to draw attention to these larger structural problems.

Then, as suddenly as the moment had begun, it was gone.

The change went further than the topic simply disappearing from the public consciousness as the DEI departments disappeared from the corporate org charts; state legislatures across the United States began to pass laws banning racial education from curricula. Suddenly, it was the DEI departments themselves that had created race and racism and "wokeness," that ill-defined term flung out at any mention of racism, especially when prefaced by "systemic." DEI became the most important, controversial issue, discussed ad nauseam by cultural commentators. Just as the Civil Rights Movement had been met with Nixon's Southern strategy and racist dog whistles, Trumpism rode the backlash to Black Lives Matter to become *the* dominant force in American politics. As America was at the cusp of recognizing its past sins, the repeating rhythm of racial backlash began blaming those who were talking about the problem for having created the controversy in the first place. It is difficult to observe the phenomenon of systemic racism, which caused and still perpetuates the racial wealth gap and myriad other racial disparities, because systemic racism is part of the system itself. Or put another way: it is impossible to understand anything about American history fully without seeing the ways that the system was built on racism. I began studying Black-owned banks in 2012 as part of my larger work to understand the nature of banking and credit. The project led to a book (*The Color of Money*) and an enlarged understanding of how government credit and banking policies produced the racial wealth gap that exists in America today. In other words, government credit and banking policies are the "systemic racism" of which people speak.

Studying Black-owned banks throughout history reveals the mechanism through which "the system" of money and credit oppresses and exploits Black communities. Once programmed, systemic racism is like an algorithm that can shape outcomes on its own—perpetually compounding the wealth of a small minority while keeping the majority impoverished. Yet to point out this truth is to face political backlash. The "system" protects itself. Its inherent inequality is blamed on Black communities' excessive spending, waste, or even their biological or cultural inferiority. This, too, is systemic racism. From the country's founding, American politics has been built on a compromise between rich white men and poor white men that gives the latter racial and gender dominion in exchange for taking a smaller stake in the venture. That political compromise is a throughline in the nation's history,

running from a founding Constitution built on slavery, to the failure
of Reconstruction, to the New Deal, to Nixon's Southern strategy, to
today's MAGA realignment of American politics.

The money-extraction machine of capitalism did not need Black
people to be poor to function. American politics did. Racism was not
just a problem to be dealt with historically; often, it was the solution to
another problem—usually an uprising that threatened to topple a social
order built on mass inequality. When white and Black sharecroppers
joined together to pose a threat to the cotton oligarchy during Reconstruction, for example, racism was deployed skillfully to break apart
the coalition. Likewise, during the 1960s, the Civil Rights Movement
became a poor people's movement aligned with the global revolutions
against colonial empire, threatening America's corporate interests.
Racism was again weaponized to create a backlash to perceived "favoritism" and "affirmative action."

Yet the story is much more complex than that of a system imposed
from the top down on Black communities. Black business and banking
have been held dear by Black leaders and activists throughout American history. In Booker T. Washington's mind, the success of Black
banks and businesses would lead to white acceptance. To Malcolm X,
Marcus Garvey, and the Black Panthers, success in this arena would
allow for Black sovereignty. Many American presidents, too, saw these
institutions as the key to Black economic health. But in practice, these
institutions are inextricable from what has always been—and, tragically, continues to be—a segregated economy.

By studying the headwinds these Black banks faced, I began to
understand something about the mechanism of systemic racism as it
applied to wealth creation. In simpler terms, I began to see how the
wealth gap was not an accidental by-product of these legal structures

but their aim. Black communities in America never stood a chance to build wealth, insofar as they lived in a violently racist state that perpetually stood in the way of progress. Even when Black communities triumphed despite the fierce forces of racism inscribed in law, they suffered the jealousy of the white-dominated system. Inevitably, violence would ensue—as it did in Tulsa, Oklahoma, in 1921.

After each blow from the law (*Dred Scott, Plessy v. Ferguson*, the New Deal with white America), the Black community had to endure being lectured by academics and policymakers, who offered one theory after another about how Black people deserved their poverty because they didn't understand "free-market capitalism" or were not good at the game, when in fact it was rigged against them. Having tipped the playing field, the white elite moralized about the laziness of those who couldn't surmount every obstacle they had thrown at them.

In the research that led to this book, I set out to explore those theories: Christian doctrine, social Darwinism, and neoliberal economics, too. Ultimately, I concluded that it is in fact the myths and stories we tell about capitalism that present the biggest obstacle to overcoming racial inequality. It is these myths that blame Black people for a problem that is systemic, that are the obstacle to justice writ large—not just for Black communities but for all Americans. For systemic racism can also be defined as an unjust system upheld and bolstered by racism. The racial wealth gap is one symptom of a massive societal wealth gap that is increasing by the day, as the top 1 percent control an ever-growing majority of the nation's wealth and the 99 percent drown under mounting debts.

Bogus notions such as social Darwinism's "scientific" racial hierarchies and the "theory" of divine right have, in America's past, attempted to justify inequality. There was also the theory that racial injustice was the "natural" result of a free market, and thus the only proper response was more capitalism. Although the myth preexisted him, Nixon called this program of evasion "Black capitalism." Instead of civil rights and equality, "Black capitalism" effectively—and by design—displaced any efforts toward integration and the amelioration of Black poverty, and every president who came after Nixon riffed on the same fundamentally flawed platform. Ironically, Black capitalism is the predecessor of today's DEI bureaucracy and the introduction of categories of minority-owned businesses, the bugaboo of the modern Right. But this was also by design. Nixon and the powerful elite who were his benefactors used Black capitalism and the affirmative action programs that accompanied it as a political weapon to stir up enough racial division to break the power of labor unions.

Black capitalism, affirmative action, and DEI programs did not just serve as a renewable source of energy, powering the culture wars and distracting Americans from the alarming concentration of wealth in ever fewer hands. They enabled the Nixon administration and those that followed to avoid the issues Black Americans very much face every day: generational poverty, segregation, and the myriad catastrophic and interrelated effects of both. Black capitalism was counterfeit capitalism—capitalism in rhetoric alone. It worked brilliantly as a credo of evasion: if the free market is responsible for the value and cost of Black labor, property, and credit, then America's legacy of exploitation, exclusion, disenfranchisement, and abuse can be ignored. If Black people are poor, per neoliberal ideology, it must be because they don't work hard enough or are irresponsible with their money. The system is not racist; rather, it is a free market that rewards all based on their own hard work and skill.

The same is true of the DEI bureaucracy today, which is a direct outgrowth of Black capitalism: it does nothing to address the root causes of the racial wealth gap while giving the illusion that special treatment is being handed out to minorities. The truth, of course, is that the violent conditions under which Black men and women were brought to America—and the subsequent legal conditions under which they have lived—are at the root of the racial wealth gap. But in soil that has been tilled for so long with racism and white supremacy, the free-market rhetoric quickly put down roots. President Bill Clinton's relabeling of America's ghettos as "enterprise zones," for instance, did precipitate an influx of investment—in the form of subprime lending. And after decades of exclusion from the housing market, the ghetto was ripe for the harvest. The results could be seen in Wells Fargo's systematic exploitation of the impoverished communities of Baltimore and beyond. The subprime mortgage crisis caused what one congressman called "a mass extinction event," wiping out 53 percent of the Black community's wealth. As Wall Street was bailed out and quickly returned to making unprecedented profits, Black communities remained vulnerable.

White-dominated institutions have not only perpetuated Black poverty and exclusion; in many instances, they have benefited from it. Slavery, sharecropping, Jim Crow segregation, affirmative action programs for white Americans, redlining, white flight patterns, and discrimination at every level of society institutionalized and reinforced anti-Black racism from America's inception, bringing with it less overt but equally destructive patterns of segregation and poverty. The racial wealth gap is one such measurement, reflecting the intertwining of race and economics in American history, but it is an important one. Wealth is where the seeds of past injustice bear fruit in present suffering. The wealth gap is not the direct cause of the deaths of George Floyd or

Michael Brown or Freddie Gray or Breonna Taylor or Eric Garner or Tamir Rice, but it is the background, setting, and context that helps explain why their lives were taken so carelessly. It is also the reason why COVID, a color-blind virus, took proportionally so many more Black lives, why environmental disasters often hit Black communities the hardest, and why health and education outcomes differ so drastically across the races.

For some people, the word "wealth" refers to a hoard of money in a bank account or a fancy car or a luxury vacation. But those are just the trappings of wealth—mere consumption. The true measure of wealth is how it shapes the world you live in. Wealth determines where people live, what schools their kids attend, whether there are parks or police stations in their neighborhoods, and whether their bodies are seen as vulnerable human bodies in need of protection or as a threat to those called to protect them. The wealth gap translates directly into an opportunity gap, a health gap, an income gap, a gap that determines practically all life outcomes that happen to correlate with race, but also with zip codes and the number of check-cashing outlets versus full-service banks one lives near. The racial wealth gap is encoded into the DNA of housing, schooling, policing, and the scarcity or abundance of access to clean air, water, and basic safety. This is another way of seeing the "system" that racism has wrought.

The explanations for the large wealth gap between races—some of whom were once legally the property of the other—are not mysterious. Many excellent scholars, past and present, have described, cataloged, and measured the effects of the aforementioned slavery, segregation, redlining, and so on. But history and data offer only partial snapshots, fixed to incomplete measurements. By providing a broad-strokes overview of the key programs and policies that helped shape the modern landscape of racial inequality, this book will shed light on the forces of debt and credit, the scaffolding shaping the invisible "system" of racism, of which the racial wealth gap is but one crucial feature. The blunter forces of violence, law, and ideology that created the racial wealth gap have not disappeared. Rather, they continue to evolve and adapt to changing times in a symbiotic coevolution of culture, law, and power.

For to say that a racial wealth gap exists—as well as a gender wealth gap—alludes to a situation in which wealth is a neutral and natural commodity that can be spread evenly among races. In fact, wealth is a legal creation; the law determines whether a piece of land or a digital abstraction has a value that can be traded on a given market. Between 1776 and 1865, the law of this nation determined that Black men and women could be tradable assets counted as wealth on a balance sheet. The law held that Native Americans could not sell property, because their "inherent savagery" barred them from property ownership. Laws determined that women, though not property, could not own property, either—nor could women have credit cards or bank accounts without their husband's permission until the passage of the 1974 Equal Credit Opportunity Act (ECOA). With so many of us being the first or second generation legally permitted to own wealth, is it any wonder that wealth gaps exist across race and gender?

Understanding the racial wealth gap requires us to challenge the basic myths upon which dominant neoliberal economics is based. These include: that money, markets, and trade exist outside the realm of political power; that inequality is a natural by-product of market forces, rather than being *created* by the state; and that people left outside the structures of power can overcome these barriers through self-help solutions or local institutions. The reality of American history is a pattern of subsidies creating white wealth, laws leading to the destruction of Black wealth, and a moral ideology that projected blame on Black communities for their lack of wealth and power. Free markets ostensibly offer an equal opportunity to trade and prosper based on one's skill and ability to produce. Yet history reveals that, in fact, markets *do* discriminate—or, alternatively, that the American economy has never borne any resemblance to a free market. To what extent could a Black property owner in the Jim Crow South rely on courts or the police to protect his property from being taken by a lynch mob or the local Klan?

Money, likewise, is said to be apolitical. As Christine Desan explains, the revisionist history of money likened it to water—neutral and colorless—flowing outside the infrastructures of power. But, in fact, money and power were in cahoots, insofar as the system of money creation was attached to a political order built on a racial hierarchy. In each historic moment when wealth was being created, whether through the Homestead Acts or Federal Housing Administration (FHA) mortgage credit, Black communities were shut out of land and wealth accumulation. Moreover, at key pivot points in history—specifically Reconstruction and the civil rights era—Black communities demanded state intervention and capital to remedy past injustices, and the rhetoric of free-market capitalism was used as a weapon to stymie their efforts.

In reality, it is fair to say that the only Americans who have ever experienced free-market capitalism—without government subsidies, free land, guaranteed loans, or legal favoritism—are Black people.

CHAPTER 1

From Capital to Capitalists

▪   ▪   ▪   ▪   ▪   ▪   ▪

S LAVERY WAS THE SCAFFOLDING UPON which the American economic system was constructed, and its legacy continues to undergird modern American capitalism. The "blood drawn with a lash" flowed into the country from its founding, priming it for a ruthless practice of capitalism that would eventually help it secure worldwide economic dominance. The economic affordances of slavery were undeniable. Slaves produced cotton, and cotton yielded profit, which increased demand for slaves, which precipitated more legislation supporting slavery. Across the globe, the clamor for cotton swelled, and America delivered. Policymakers, courts, and citizens alike supported and enforced the abusive, exploitative institution. Built upon this barbaric structure, American commerce flourished, delivering unparalleled bounty to the developing nation.

Slaves were not just the generators of cotton production. They were the collateral used to finance the institution. The market value of slavery—four million slaves were worth $4 billion before the Civil War—was almost equal to the entire gross national product of the

United States. Black men and women became the capital and the labor enriching the U.S. economy. The legal code of the nation converted human bodies into assets, credit, and debt instruments, ones easier to exchange on markets than other forms of property. Between 1820 and the Civil War, Confederate banks across the South issued notes with images of slaves printed on the money. Slavery modernized credit markets, creating complex new financial instruments and trade networks through which slaves could be mortgaged, exchanged, and used as leverage to purchase more slaves. Americans and the British built fortunes on slavery and defended the institution with law and violence, with the British developing the common law on contracts to protect their overseas investments.

Perhaps because of these obvious economic benefits, and despite being antithetical to the values professed in America's founding documents, Americans not only tolerated but embraced the institution. Insidious rationalizations took root, including baseless theories of racial hierarchy and distortions of Christian principles. In order for the treatment of human beings as chattel to mesh with the principles America professed to hold dear, Americans had to distort their perceptions. They had to view Black people as inherently below whites—as subhuman. During the antebellum period, the media aided and abetted this distortion, creating and perpetuating ideas of Black inferiority that, unfortunately, persist to this day. Christianity contributed mightily as well. Racial subjugation and white supremacy were sanctioned under the notion that God not only condoned the system but willed it to be so. As one Presbyterian minister pontificated in *The Christian Doctrine of Slavery*, "It may be that *Christian slavery* is God's solution of the problem [that is, the relation of labor and capital] about which the wisest of statesmen of Europe confess themselves 'at fault.'" If it had been decreed by God that whites should suck capital from Black labor, what mere mortal possessed the authority to suggest otherwise? These psychological, philosophical, and intellectual attempts to justify slavery warped the floorboards of the early American psyche as they were laid; that foundational damage is present today, in society and the economy alike. Because slavery was such a crucial component of economic prosperity—and had been long before America gained independence—it follows that a racial wealth disparity was woven into the founding of this country.

The struggle for freedom and democracy during Reconstruction was a struggle not between white and Black but between democracy and empire. Specifically, paying a fair wage for labor on the cotton plantations would have—per the law of supply and demand—increased the price of cotton, which would have threatened the profits not just of the Southern oligarchs but of the bankers, traders, and investors in the worldwide cotton market that linked the plantations of the South to New York, London, Liverpool, and India. These investors had built an empire on cheap cotton exports, and they did everything in their power to restore cotton prices to their prewar levels as soon as the bloodiest war in our nation's history was over. The first threat to cotton prices was the proposal to give freedmen a stake in the land they had tilled as slaves.

Upon emancipation, Black leaders went to Union military leaders with the proposition that in order to achieve and maintain self-reliance in America, Black people must be extended the opportunity to work on their own land and establish communities by their own labor. Eventually, Union general William T. Sherman set aside four hundred thousand acres of confiscated land for ex-slaves, and President Abraham Lincoln's Congress created the Freedmen's Bureau for distributing land. The Freedmen's Bureau Act of 1865 solidified Sherman's initiative, promising forty acres of inexpensive land on credit. Some families also received an old army mule. The act caused rabid backlash from the white South, including the rise of the Ku Klux Klan as a military force bent on overthrowing anyone who questioned restoring the antebellum way.

Andrew Johnson's first act in office in 1866, after President Lincoln was assassinated, was to veto the bill and the land grant (except one provision)—instructing the freedmen that, now that the law had transformed them from capital to capitalists, they needed nothing but freedom of contract and a free market to participate in capitalism. This was either unbelievably naïve or incredibly cynical. For as far as the cotton markets were concerned, the freedmen of the South could not be allowed to go the way of the freedmen in Haiti, who, after ejecting their enslavers, had decided to diversify their crops, growing less of the cash crop (sugar) and more of what they could eat and trade.

Insisting that America would retain a "white man's government," Johnson collapsed Lincoln's promises and set about returning the land granted by the Freedmen's Bureau Act of 1865 to its original owners. His justification for doing so was that the recipients should have to pay for the land, that the act went against free-market principles, and that it unfairly advantaged Black people. His administration operated under the assumption that free trade and capitalism would function as designed, like a clock wound by an omnipotent clockmaker, and that Black people would be able to reap the benefits of these systems without government assistance. Other government programs, like the Homestead Acts, which doled out millions of acres of free land to white settlers, did not receive the same condemnation and were upheld.

Not only did Johnson's administration return the confiscated land; officials welcomed Southern rebels back into the nation and the economy with open arms. Such actions were instrumental in reinforcing the slap-on-the-wrist punishments for racist actions that have endured from the founding of the nation to this day.

The Southern economy was nothing like a free market. Whites refused to sell property to Black people. Southern legislators, lawyers, and judges drafted laws governing every aspect of Black labor. They restricted Black people from skilled trade. Vagrancy laws were prevalent. Wages were capped by law and by cabal between the employers. And violations led to convict labor without due process. Jim Crow laws, the underpinnings of which began in the North long before the Civil War, plunged free Black people into a second, far-less-than-equal America, effectively blocking their engagement with the white-dominated economy. "Black Codes" in the South prohibited Black people from owning property, participating in commercial trade, testifying in courts, suing white debtors, or becoming members of thrift, building, or loan institutions. Rationalized by claims that Southern society depended on Black labor, these actions ensured economic stagnation for Black farmers. Even the few who managed to save diligently faced prohibitive laws against Black landownership. Concrete legislation, coupled with pervasive racism, rendered social mobility nearly impossible.

Reconstruction, W.E.B. Du Bois argued, was a successful interracial democracy violently suppressed. Only after its destruction did Jim Crow laws formalize what the Confederacy had failed to achieve in battle: the subjugation of Black Americans through forced labor. Northern interests supported the return to an antebellum-like system, citing the national economy's reliance on cheap Black labor. Although the Fifteenth Amendment granted Black men the right to vote, it did nothing to address the widening economic disparities. As James Baldwin aptly put it, Reconstruction was "a bargain between the North and South to this effect: 'We've liberated them from the land—and delivered them to the bosses.'"

BY THE END OF the Reconstruction era, most freedmen were left landless, voteless, and with practically every profession blocked to them; their only choice was to grow cotton. Of course, that was the point. In order for the country to have enough cotton exports, the freedmen had to grow it. And for that to happen, they could not be landowners. It was the cotton market's demand for cheap cotton that stole the promise of democracy—not a so-called commitment to free-market capitalism.

Cotton was still the country's largest export—the country made two billion pounds of it in 1860. New England mills consumed over 280 million pounds of cotton per year, up to 70 percent of which came from the slavery South. Southern cotton was Great Britain's largest import, and the cotton mills and looms in Liverpool that had fueled the industrial booms in both countries remained hungry. Britain, still the world's ruling empire, relied on cotton from the American South for over 80 percent of its raw materials, according to historian Gene Dattel. And the textiles that Britain's mills produced made up 40 percent of their total exports, employing a fifth of the population—the wealthiest nation in the world thus deriving most of its wealth from the plantations they had built in their former colony.

Independence or not, the financial legacy of empire had not been broken. "King Cotton" was the slogan that convinced the Confederacy to secede, the reasoning being that Great Britain would surely come to their aid, reliant as they were on cotton. It did not have to come to that. As Sven Beckert's comprehensive history of the era, *Empire of Cotton*, explains, during the Civil War the cotton capitalists "saw promising new levers that might move the mountain of free labor into cotton cultivation with new lands, new labor relations, and new connections between them." They learned that their lucrative empire could be "protected and maintained by unprecedented state activism." As a French observer noted, "The empire of cotton is ensured; King Cotton is not dethroned."

The merchants and bankers from the old-world empire continued their dominance by extracting their wealth from the plantations and the brutal system of slavery, which their legislatures had made a point of denouncing. When they were forced to give up their plantations, as the French were after the Haitian revolution, they did so only by extracting reparations from the freed slaves—hundreds of billions of dollars of compensation over hundreds of years.

Just as the new system of debt extracted forced labor from more or less the same people who had just been freed from chains, so too did the wealth made from the empire of cotton remain, more or less, in the same hands as before. The laws of primogeniture no longer strictly held that a father's property went to his eldest son, but the wealth still tended to flow in that direction. In fact, as Claudio Saunt has shown in the context of stolen Indigenous land, as Douglas Blackmon has shown in terms of post-emancipation convict leasing, and as Thomas Piketty has shown in terms of the reparations extracted from Haitians, the wealth that was taken by brutality, exploitation, and theft remains, growing in the coffers of wealthy heirs and modern corporations.

———

So LONG AS THE British had the world's store of gold and demanded worldwide exchange using the gold standard, the financial pull of empire was strong and centripetal. To truly free Americans once and for all from the tyranny of empire required a reckoning with the monetary standard. This was what Lincoln was up to with the issue of greenbacks, the nation's first fiat currency. Had he survived and been able to see the project through, the story of Reconstruction might have played out differently. As it happened, the half century after the Civil War saw a political divide centered on escaping the gold standard—to set farmers and laborers free from the scarcity that impoverished and indebted the majority of Americans. American financiers would be the forceful opposition.

Most of the wealth, as wealth does, continued to flow in the same direction—toward financial markets in New York and London, where it could seek yield in finance and banking enterprises. Modern behemoths like Lloyd's of London, Barclays, and Royal Bank of Scotland arose atop the slave economy, and the wealth in notes and bonds, credit and debt such institutions extracted persisted for centuries. Bankers even used that capital to finance the war itself. The American John Pierpont Morgan turned cotton wealth into a weapons fortune—he earned the epithet "robber baron" for his controversial swindle of the Union, the Hall Carbine Affair: Morgan financed a shipment of 5,000 rifles at $3.50 each headed for the Union army, then confiscated them and sold them to the government at $22 apiece. A congressional committee investigating the affair in 1863 reported, "Worse than traitors in arms are the men who pretending loyalty to the flag, feast and fatten on the misfortunes of the nation, while patriot blood is crimsoning the plains of the South and bodies of their countrymen are moldering in the dust." The affair caused little lasting harm to Morgan, who a half century later was the wealthiest man in the world. In other words, though the war was long and bloody, the gold came out clean on the other side.

RECONSTRUCTION AIMED TO RECTIFY the original sin of slavery, yet the period was marked by instability. The bankers, merchants, and plantation owners north and south and east and west still worshipped King Cotton. Seeing the Reconstruction era from the seat of the cotton empire is to see that no matter the politics of the thing, the Southern plantations had to be turned back on to produce cheap and abundant cotton. Black participation in American capitalism proved to be an illusion. The economic system of the cotton-producing South shifted from plantation labor coerced through torture and violence called slavery to a system of labor coerced through debt contracts and violence that the elites called "capitalism." Academics refer to it as "sharecropping." Often the people kept in bondage remained on the same plantation where they'd been enslaved, but rather than tangible chains, abstract chains of debt bound them to the land.

The system worked like this: sharecroppers would rent a parcel of land, seeds, equipment, and basic provisions from the landlord, whose system of weights and measures could not be challenged without fear of violence. The master and overseer gave way to the merchant and creditor, described by Du Bois as "part banker, part despot." The sharecropper had to grow enough cotton not only to pay the rent for the equipment and seeds but to provide for all their other goods with the income gained from selling their cotton back to the banker-despot-landlord (a.k.a. "the market"). Some years, the profits barely exceeded the costs. In other years, they did not, and the debt would mount. Du Bois later labeled sharecropping "a system of peonage that kept [Black people] in debt virtually from cradle to grave."

TO ESCAPE PERPETUAL POVERTY, sharecroppers planted more cotton, but this left little room for subsistence farming, so the sharecropping family's entire well-being was connected to the cotton market. And the more the sharecroppers grew, the lower the prices for the worldwide cotton trade plunged, which meant that each sharecropper had to grow even more, in a self-destructive loop that put self-advancement at odds with collective well-being. It was a lose-lose situation for those who grew cotton and a win-win for those who purchased it—the latter being the group that had devised the system by denying the freedmen land.

These elite interests and their representatives had taken up seats on the courts and legislatures, thanks to the total disenfranchisement of Black Southerners through poll taxes and tests. Thus, the men who wrote the laws and enforced them held the maintenance of the sharecropping system of labor that enriched them as their top priority. A Black litigant had no legal recourse in Southern courts for challenging any contractual arrangement. Noncompliance was punished by the disproportionate violence of the state or the paramilitary violence of the Klan. Not only that: thanks to the "Black Codes" mentioned above, the sharecropper could not choose to do anything besides sharecropping— could not gather income for skilled work of any kind, could not join a profession or simply refuse to work. Any violation of these laws led to prison, another antebellum innovation that bore an uncanny resemblance to slavery: convicts were forced to work in mines and factories, many until they were injured or died from overwork.

By 1870, Southern cotton exports had returned to prewar levels, and by 1891, production had doubled. The breach between North and South healed, and Reconstruction's political upheaval ended, but at the cost of Black freedom and dreams of an equitable monetary and credit system. During Reconstruction, former slaves had become members of Congress, disrupting entrenched racial hierarchies. But, while not inevitable, racism's toxic power reasserted itself.

In the 1890s, following a particularly severe recession, the Populist Party sought to break the cycle of debt in the South by uniting Black sharecroppers and white yeomen farmers. Its members recognized that white supremacy and racial animosity were tools used to divide and oppress poor Americans. For a brief moment, hope for an alliance between poor Black and white people sparked. Ultimately, though, the entrenched ideology of racial hierarchy extinguished it. Historians like Du Bois, C. Vann Woodward, and Eric Foner have chronicled these dynamics. Efforts to unite Black and white laborers against the exploitative sharecropping system threatened elite interests. In response, Southern Democrats weaponized white supremacy to divide and suppress these movements, reinstating racial superiority as a basis for power.

After the failure of Reconstruction, the only tangible legacy of the Freedmen's Act of 1865 was a bank—instead of getting land, the freed slaves were admonished to turn to "thrift and savings" to "earn" it instead. The act had established a savings bank for Black people, called the Freedman's Savings and Trust Company—the first and only savings bank ever founded by the federal government. It was marketed as the most respectable way for Black people to save their wages. Because many Black people were employed by the Freedman's Bank, some Black leaders saw it as a scaffolding for future Black banking.

They argued that it provided Black people with firsthand experience in finance. Moreover, the experience of working at, or simply engaging with, a bank felt like a giant step forward, a stark contrast to the barbaric experience of slavery.

The Freedman's Savings Bank was riddled with issues. Since it was designed for saving, not for lending or investing, there was no real potential for capital growth. It was deregulated and essentially looted by its chair, Henry Cooke, and other white managers. Slowly, these men transformed the Freedman's Savings Bank into a highly speculative investment bank aimed to line their own pockets. The collected savings of the Black community—earned through their toil in the punitive sharecropping economy—amounted to $1.5 billion in today's dollar values. Henry Cooke handed the money to his brother, Jay Cooke, an infamous Wall Street speculator, who fed it into the maw of Wall Street's lucrative yet risky bond market, which was connected and indeed fed by that same extractive labor economy. Jay Cooke lost that bet, but the debt that beggared farmers and sharecroppers across the nation would make a few men unimaginable riches. This would translate, in turn, into political power, which these men used to keep the system that fed on racism and poverty intact.

The Freedman's Savings Bank eventually failed, despite the last-minute appointment of Frederick Douglass as president. Many freed Black people lost their savings entirely, a disastrous and demoralizing blow to those who had been so diligently socking away their meager earnings. Suddenly they found themselves with nothing to show for their work, or for their trust in the government. Bank failures caused by runs are the underbelly of capitalism: the deposits, there one minute, are gone the next—disappeared through the sorcery of speculation. Perhaps the largest casualty of the bank's folding was the loss of faith, among freed Black people, in the American government and financial institutions. The incident served as a stark reminder that Black Americans were not yet in charge of their economic destiny. As Du Bois put it, "Not even ten additional years of slavery could have done so much to throttle the thrift of the freedmen as the mismanagement and bankruptcy of the series of savings banks chartered by the Nation for their special aid."

THOUGH THE FIFTEENTH AMENDMENT had been in place since 1870, granting voting rights to all men, independent of their race, Southern politicians of the late 1800s worked hard to keep Black men from the polls. They devised myriad laws and strategies to ensure the continuation of white supremacy, such as literacy tests and property-ownership requirements, complete with "grandfathering" clauses to allow poor, uneducated whites to bypass tests designed to exclude Black men. Before long, the rights bestowed by the Thirteenth, Fourteenth, and Fifteenth Amendments were meticulously stripped away again.

Racial hierarchy was instrumental in maintaining the economic boom afforded by Black field labor. Dehumanizing rhetoric, a sharp tool for this endeavor, was pervasive. One Missouri congressman, David A. DeArmond, called Black people "almost too ignorant to eat, scarcely wise enough to breathe, mere existing human machines." Senator James K. Vardaman of Mississippi proclaimed that he was "just as much opposed to Booker Washington as a voter, with all his Anglo-Saxon re-enforcements, as [he was] to the coconut-headed, chocolate-colored, typical little coon, Andy Dotson, who black[ed his] shoes every morning. Neither is fit to exercise the supreme function of citizenship." Philosopher Hannah Arendt called such race-thinking a "political weapon," and so it was in the South.

Black franchise would be stripped through loopholes and legal technicalities for another hundred years—until Martin Luther King Jr., flanked by Lincoln's ghost, pleaded for the restoration of the promise of emancipation. The actual amendments—the Thirteenth, Fourteenth, and Fifteenth—could not be revoked short of another war, but neither would the Southern elite or the worldwide cotton trade tolerate a landowning population of freed men. Resubjugation of the recently freed required a revisionist history, and one was provided by a "lost cause narrative" absolving the slaveholders and by new myths of Black criminality that sought to justify "slavery by another name."

The United States Supreme Court readily joined the South in enforcing the racial order. In an effort to mediate the federal and state tensions that had escalated since the Civil War, the Supreme Court continued to undermine the ability of Black people to contest racism. Several decisions made between 1873 and 1898 diminished federal oversight and gave states more power over the treatment of their citizens. Perhaps the most destructive of these decisions, *Plessy v. Ferguson*, codified the flagrantly untrue doctrine of "separate but equal." *Plessy v. Ferguson* legitimized Jim Crow laws and segregation for half a century, during which time the carefully worked disparities—economic, social, and political—between Black and white people would grow even more profoundly sedimented.

Jim Crow laws quickly became part of the American landscape. Bathrooms, work sites, entrances and exits, stairways, and water fountains—among many other heretofore commonly used spaces and fixtures—were segregated. Black people were swiftly cut out of white American life. Southern courts and law enforcement sprang into action, too, building on the oppression of the Black race in every way possible. White terrorism and violence, to which the eye of the law remained intentionally blind, battered the Black community incessantly, until "Southern trees bore strange fruit, / Blood on the leaves and blood at the root."

The failure of Reconstruction was not inevitable. Nor was the revival of white supremacy, the creation of the Klan, or the reassertion of white domination through Jim Crow laws and the debt-peonage system of sharecropping. White supremacy triumphed because of its electoral appeal to Southern white voters, the North's abdication, the cotton market's demands, and various legislative and judicial actions. Before Black men were reenslaved and the history of Reconstruction was revised to make its demise a foregone conclusion, democracy was *tried*, and it was tried for almost a decade. It was, as Du Bois wrote, "the finest effort to achieve democracy for the working millions which this world had ever seen." The Black community and their many allies struggled heroically as soldiers, workers, voters, teachers, activists, organizers, and elected officials in legislatures to achieve full equality and to claim their freedom. Indeed, freedom and equality were imaginable for the first time in American history.

"The slave went free; stood a brief moment in the sun; then moved back again toward slavery," lamented Du Bois. Is it naïve to see that things could have gone another way? Perhaps. But because of this historic effort and its subversion, the new order of racial oppression had to be imposed on different terms.

CHAPTER 2

The Evolution of the Race Problem

IN THE MIDST OF A worldwide market that produced cotton wealth for the merchants and unsustainable debt and oppression for the sharecroppers, freed Black people created self-governing communities, attempting to raise their economic status through joint-stock companies and the patronization of Black businesses. By the 1900s, it had become clear that to be successful in business and advance themselves in a capitalist economy, they had to establish their own banking system. Black-owned lending systems started privately, with wealthier Black men lending money to less financially stable members of the community. More formal banking was conducted through churches—though attempts were made to thwart the collective power of these institutions—or philanthropic organizations.

These early efforts at Black banking were met with challenges. Chief among them were lack of capital—due, in part, to political powerlessness—and lack of support from the federal government, which resulted in extreme difficulty securing credit. A catch-22 began that perseveres today: in order to build capital, Black people needed bank credit; in order to establish a bank—and therefore bank credit—capital was necessary.

As they worked on developing their own financial sphere, financial and economic slavery persisted in measurable ways, even for those who had been freed. Jim Crow laws stifled economic participation. Freed Black people were expected to become full-fledged capitalists overnight, despite having virtually no capital, property, or other resources—nor avenues by which to attain them.

FROM THE BEGINNING OF American history, race was an instrument of oppression, exploitation, and marginalization. If there was a silver lining to that ominous black cloud, though, it was that around the turn of the twentieth century, race also started to become the nexus around which a vibrant community, a unique cultural identity, and racial solidarity began to form. Fraternal societies, charities, travel agencies, and Black holidays like Juneteenth and National Freedom Day cropped up across the nation. In the words of contemporary Black thinker and activist Ta-Nehisi Coates: "They made us into a race. We made ourselves into a people."

Churches resided at the heart of mutual aid and fraternal societies, working to support and advance the Black community. This connection between church and bank was a blessing and a curse. While being attached to a central community pillar provided support to banks, it also brought the complications and risks of business into one of the few spaces in which Black people were allowed to build community. Black clients sometimes expected Black banks to treat them as friends rather than customers or even debtors.

The Grand United Order of True Reformers in Richmond, Virginia, was a more sophisticated financial organization. It opened the first formal Black bank, the True Reformers Bank, which offered something akin to formal insurance policies. "If we had a bank of our own," suggested the order, "the white people would not have any information about our activities." Though the True Reformers Bank survived a rash of financial troubles and was dubbed the "Gibraltar of Negro Business," it folded in 1910 after an attempt at expansion into commercial lending.

One of the most remarkable achievements in Black banking came at the hands of Maggie Walker, the first Black woman to own a bank in the United States and the second woman of any race to do so. Daughter to a former slave and an Irish Confederate soldier, she was raised in abject poverty by her mother. Walker began her rise to success by pulling the Order of St. Luke's mutual aid society from a downward spiral. She went on to establish a newspaper, a printing press, an insurance company, a college education fund, and the St. Luke Penny Savings Bank. In all her endeavors, she strove to uplift Black people—specifically Black women. "The great all absorbing interest, the thing which has driven sleep from my eyes and fatigue from my body," she said, "is the love I bear women, our Negro women, hemmed in, circumscribed with every imaginable obstacle in our way, blocked and held down by the fears and prejudices of the whites—ridiculed and sneered at by the intelligent blacks." It was said of Walker that "if the State of Virginia had done no more, in fifty years, with the funds spent on the education of the Negroes than to educate Mrs. Walker, the State would have been amply repaid for its outlays and efforts."

The Jim Crow economy necessitated Black-run financial institutions, but it also hindered them incalculably. These institutions were mired in the same dilemma as was Black leadership, which James Baldwin described as "the nicely refined torture [of] having been created and defeated by the same circumstances."

Booker T. Washington and W.E.B. Du Bois each faced this same dilemma. Though they were both proponents of Black banking, they had dramatically different blueprints for Black progress; Washington centered the development of a segregated Black community, whereas Du Bois insisted on full integration and equal rights.

Washington's rise to prominence began in 1895, after a speech dubbed "The Atlanta Compromise," in which he seemingly endorsed segregation. Addressing a largely white audience, Washington decreed that "in all things that are purely social we can be as separate as the fingers, yet one as the hand in all things essential to mutual progress." His adherence to segregation—to say nothing of his fervent belief in the capitalist "gospel of prosperity"—fit neatly into the vision of America held by the white establishment; indeed, he was frequently praised by the white elite. He was convinced that capitalism would favor Black business as readily as it favored wealthy whites like Andrew Carnegie and John D. Rockefeller. Washington's stature in the post-Reconstruction era allowed his staunchly pro-capitalist stance to shape generations of leaders and businessmen, both Black and white. Because of his important and influential position in the Black community, his belief in the efficacy of "Black capitalism" might well have limited other potentially more promising developments in Black economic prosperity.

In retrospect, Washington's faith that Black wealth would foster white acceptance was, tragically, misguided. By the turn of the twentieth century, racism was an inextricable part of the American design. To white supremacist Thomas Dixon, for example, Washington's efforts to help Black people become financially independent was a flagrant violation of Southern ideology, which held that "the Negro remain[ed] on this continent for one reason only . . . the Southern white man has needed his labor." Though Washington believed that public sentiment in the South was progressing, rhetoric like Dixon's and that of the Ku Klux Klan was only just getting started.

Unlike Washington, who was born enslaved in the South, W.E.B. Du Bois was born free in the North. Armed with a Harvard PhD and a passion just as fervent as—albeit radically different from—Washington's, Du Bois urged Black people not to rest until full legal rights and integration had been attained. A co-founder of the National Association for the Advancement of Colored People (NAACP), Du Bois set out to pry America from Jim Crow's vise grip. Du Bois was staunchly supportive of Black business, though he was unflinchingly critical of capitalism, warning against the notion of "wealth as a remedy for every social ill."

Providing labor, which translated into capital for white America, was not only insufficient for Black advancement; it was a sure way to cement the racial wealth divide permanently. In order to build meaningful capital, though, Black people had to extend beyond "pebbles on the shore of business enterprise," as John Hope, president of Atlanta University, put it. Until they had their own "factories, railroads and banks," Hope decreed, there could be no real chance of a thriving Black economy.

Large-scale Black enterprise remained absent from the American landscape in the early 1900s, but Black businesses continued to proliferate. Four thousand Black-owned businesses burgeoned into seventy thousand between 1867 and 1930, many of them catering to Black needs brought about by segregation. In a study of nearly two thousand Black businesses, Du Bois identified the vast majority of goods and services provided. Under this dynamic, "house servants became barbers, restaurant keepers and caterers; field hands became gardeners, grocers, florists, and mill owners. Those who had been plantation craftsmen used their talents to become builders and contractors, brick masons, painters and blacksmiths." Many of these enterprises did not last long; they were mostly individually owned, and they often died with the founder. Despite valiant effort, they failed to significantly accumulate capital for the Black community.

IN RESPONSE TO THE growing clamor to expand Black business, Booker T. Washington founded the National Negro Business League (NNBL) in 1900. With Washington at its helm, the NNBL encouraged young Black people to start businesses, and celebrated the creation of new Black banks. The NNBL even proposed a financing corporation for extending credit to Black businesses, though it never managed to amass enough capital for the endeavor.

The strong links between Black business and religion persisted. Black pastors promoted Black banks, and these banks gleaned community support from those endorsements. The historian Clifford Kuhn commented on this phenomenon as he saw it unfold in Atlanta's Citizens Trust Bank: "The preachers made Citizens Trust Bank. . . . They put in deposits that Monday morning. Around 11:00 o'clock the lobby would be full of nothing but preachers. And the people, seeing their preacher deposit God's money from the churches in Citizens Trust, put their money into it and helped to put it over, in a great way."

But the landscape of Black business in the early twentieth century was a far cry from the idyllic holy land about which Booker T. Washington proselytized. Segregation laws prevented Black businesses from reaching a white clientele, and this roadblock went only one way. White businesses could, and sometimes did, cater to Black people. Black businesses were fighting an uphill battle, competing with white businesses and other Black businesses alike.

This critical disadvantage precipitated numerous others. Black businesses struggled to grow, excluding them from the affordances of scale and making their operations more expensive. Black leaders stressed the importance of "buying Black," but Black customers who heeded this guidance found themselves purchasing inferior goods at a higher cost, due to the strictures of Jim Crow.

Of the few Black businesses that did prosper, most managed to do so by meeting a demand that white businesses would or could not address. One such instance was the entrepreneurship of Madame C. K. Walker. Walker, born Sarah Breedlove, sold hair products to Black women. The products included hair straighteners as well as tonics to remedy hair loss caused by malnutrition, stress, and incessant labor. She employed a task force of Black women, dubbed "Walker agents," to help her expand her business, and was the first Black business owner to become a self-made millionaire. Walker's success speaks as much to her own genius as it does to the headwinds others faced: not only was her business built on selling Black women hair-straightening products, which would not have been such a robust market in a world that didn't impose white supremacist beauty standards on Black women, but she had virtually no competition from white businesses. In fact, most Black businesses that succeeded in this era were in industries without white competition—for example, funeral parlors, Black life insurance, hair care, and Black banking.

Black insurance companies, designed to offer some protection against the considerable risks and difficulties Black people were up against, were essential, plentiful, and largely successful. At the time, insurance necessitated mutual trust between salesperson and customer; this dynamic was not often possible between white insurance agents and Black customers. As one scholar noted, "Nothing has more greatly aided Negro agents in meeting the competition of their more experienced competitors than the abundance of examples of insults to and abuses of Negro policyholders at the hands of white agents which could nearly always be pointed out in every community." Insidious racist notions, such as Frederick L. Hoffman's belief that the Black race was destined for extinction "not [due to] the conditions of life but [to] the race traits and tendencies," prevented many white insurers from insuring Black people. The lynching of a Black man at the hands of a white insurance agent in Mississippi validated these fears, and Black customers flocked to Black insurers.

The dream of a thriving, self-sufficient Black economy nearly came true in both Durham, North Carolina, and Tulsa, Oklahoma.

Referred to as "Negro Wall Street" and named Hayti after the first independent Black republic, the Black district in Durham was established right after the Civil War. Hayti thrummed with Black businesses, banks, and insurance companies. It was also home to two prominent Black churches and a Black college. "Go to Durham and see the industrious Negro at his best," touted one Richmond newspaper. "Go to Durham and see the cooperative spirit among Negroes at its best. Go to Durham and see Negro business with an aggregate capital of millions. Go to Durham and see twenty-two Negro men whose honesty and business sagacity are making modern history."

THE TOBACCO AND COTTON industries—both of which boomed in Durham—began to hire Black workers at the turn of the century. The availability of steady work for all citizens and the economic stability this work provided fostered inclusion. As the mayor of Durham aptly stated in an address to visiting Black bankers, "Go back home and tell your people that the whites and the blacks here are working shoulder to shoulder." Unlike in most of the rest of the country, Black businesses in Durham—particularly those manufacturing goods such as bricks, iron articles, and mattresses—attracted white customers, allowing those firms to move beyond the segregated economy and participate in the larger market. One such business, a hosiery mill, even hired white workers. This notable economic success and relative racial harmony persevered until 1958, when the state of North Carolina split the business district in two by building a freeway down the center of Hayti.

In Tulsa, though, what began as a dream swiftly became a nightmare. Business in Tulsa surged when oil was discovered nearby in 1905. Black residents, who made up 10 percent of the city's population by 1910, created their own business hub in the Greenwood District. For a time, the area grew and prospered, just as Hayti had in Durham. Oil speculation was lucrative, and made many Black businessmen wealthy.

Indeed, the Greenwood district's ultimate fate might well have been precipitated by this industry, which was reported to have escalated racial tension. One editorial from 1921 indicated that "every increase in the price of oil made the strife more bitter. With the depression of the labor market, white employers of labor at last thought they had the whip hand and ordered Negro employees to sell out or quit. Even housewives refused to continue to keep colored women in their employ."

THE PRECISE CONDITIONS FOR the violence that annihilated the Greenwood district have been difficult to pinpoint, largely due to a lack of coverage at the time. Nonetheless, most sources point to one event—the claim that a Black man had attacked a white woman in an elevator—as the trigger that set off a devastating chain reaction. The accused man, who denied culpability, was arrested, and a white lynch mob quickly formed outside the prison. Thirty armed Black men coalesced in opposition to the mob. A shot was fired into the air when one white man attempted to disarm a Black war veteran. Though the Black men backed off, the white mob was far from finished. They poured into Greenwood that night, rioting and looting, hell-bent on the desire to "burn the nigger out." They left 300 people dead, most of them Black. Many more were injured; 304 homes were looted, and 18,000 others were reduced to ash.

The thorough destruction of Black Tulsa did not end there. The National Guard arrived and moved the 6,000 displaced Black residents into camps, marching them through the streets with their hands above their heads. These individuals were made to wear identification tags, to be signed by white employers before they were able to return to work. The grand jury maintained that, though the elevator incident had sparked the riot, there existed indirect causes more vital to the public interest: "Among them were agitation among the negroes of social equality and the laxity of law enforcement." This phenomenon, wherein the majority group responds with violence to a perceived economic threat, is known as "host group dominance," and can be found at work throughout American history.

PERHAPS THE DREAM IN Durham did not end in flames, as it did in Tulsa, because the residents of Hayti were more integrated into the white population of the city and because Durham's "Negro Wall Street" was beneficial to both Black and white citizens. It is possible, too, that the lavish display of Black wealth in Tulsa sparked outrage, whereas Hayti's residents were more subdued in the manifestation of their prosperity. Regardless, white America would not allow the reverie of Black success to continue indefinitely in either place. Two truths were simultaneously becoming apparent: Black people would have to rely on themselves for economic stability, and the system of white power would fight that self-reliance tooth and nail.

BY THE EARLY 1900S, debt peonage tied to cotton production was no longer profitable enough to meet the demands of global capital. Just as the South settled into a racially stratified economic order upheld by Southern Democrats, a series of economic upheavals forced significant change. Chief among these was the Industrial Revolution, which shifted the country's economic focus from agriculture to industry, leading to the rise of urban centers and the dominance of industrial magnates. Power gravitated toward industrialists who built monopolies in steel, railroads, finance, oil, and manufacturing, all industries hungry for labor. These factories drew workers—Black and white, native-born and immigrant, male and female—into grueling cycles of production. The era was marked by violent conflicts between capitalists and laborers, including strikes and uprisings, which were often met with brutal suppression.

Into this new economic transition stepped the populist and progressive movements, which attempted to forge alliances among debtors against creditors, to join farmers and producers against Wall Street speculators, to fight monopolies through unions, cooperatives, and boycotts. Chief among the concerns that united populists and progressives was the issue of the monetary standard—specifically, they advocated moving from a gold standard to a looser monetary standard: either silver, bimetallism, or paper money. The nation had already experimented, quite successfully, with fiat money (greenbacks) during the Civil War, but Wall Street and other primarily wealthy interests demanded a return to hard money, or gold.

A money system based solely on gold benefited savers and creditors but made credit tight for farmers and debtors. Gold was scarce and thus limited the money in circulation, which favored those who already held it; according to basic economic law, the lower the supply for any good, the higher the demand. But money was not a commodity—or, rather, it was not only a commodity, and this was the problem to begin with. Gold was both money and commodity—meaning it was both the means of exchange and a source of wealth that could be hoarded. Changing the monetary standard, which could be done by fiat (i.e., law) would increase the supply of money, which would loosen up credit and allow more farmers to get loans, but it would diminish the value of the hoards of gold held by the wealthy. The debate led to a perfect political divide, with those who had on one side and those that didn't on the other. It is no wonder that the populists and progressives forged alliances among city laborers, Southern debtors, and farmers on the frontier. On the other side, unfortunately, were the most powerful and politically connected interests in the nation—those who hold the gold, goes one version of the "golden rule," get to write the rules.

Progressive leader and three-time presidential candidate William Jennings Bryan launched his 1896 campaign by bellowing, "You cannot crucify mankind on a cross of gold"—by which he meant the gold standard. The debates about money mirrored those about society and the economy and which came first. As Bryan described it, "There are two ideas of government. There are those who believe that if you just legislate to make the well-to-do prosperous, that their prosperity will leak through on those below. The Democratic idea has been that if you legislate to make the masses prosperous their prosperity will find its way up and through every class that rests upon it." The speech preceded Reagan's trickle-down economics by a century, revealing that not much has changed. But the conflict was not just about *how* resources should be distributed—it was about *who* had the right to do the distributing.

As Bryan said, if the money power belonged to the people, it should serve them all. Groups called the "free silverites" and "the greenback-ers" fought for economic equality through monetary policy. Debates about the gold standard were debates about justice and fairness and who would hold the wealth of the country. The Populist Party plat-form of 1892 was entirely about money and banking: "We demand a national currency, safe, sound, and flexible, issued by the general gov-ernment only, a full legal tender for all debts, public and private, and that without the use of banking corporations, a just, equitable, and efficient means of distribution direct to the people. . . . We demand that postal savings banks be established by the government for the safe deposit of the earnings of the people and to facilitate exchange." These movements understood that the nature of the banks that lent credit—their size, location, and ownership—was crucial to extending the reach of credit.

Debates over currency and banking continued to divide the nation—not just between North and South but between rich and poor, industrial power and plantation economies, and workers and capital-ists. Currency debates were also about the nature of society and the changeability of value. Those who argued for fiat argued that money was socially created and thus changeable, which is the same argu-ment abolitionists made—racial hierarchies were socially constructed and thus could be socially deconstructed. Those who insisted on "hard money" believed gold to be the true and natural basis of value, which was not dissimilar to the argument that race essentialists made about natural race hierarchies. Or as "hard money" proponent Enoch Powell put it, "Color is the uniform" that signals "a separate and strange population." Proponents of gold-backed currency called it "natural," "scientific," and "sound money," while fiat was the "mongrelization" of money. Gold was the divinely ordained "true" form of value. Inequality was a hard, unchangeable fact of nature.

Gold also enriched the few at the expense of the many, and was the cause of crisis after crisis. The real concern was that changes to monetary policy would disrupt or devalue the fortunes of those at the top of the financial hierarchy. Changes in the monetary standard, like inflation today, affected property and contract rights by altering the measurement of value. Those whose riches were largest under the gold standard often stood in the way of change. Eventually, Bryan's form of populist progressivism lost. The Democrats and their candidate, Woodrow Wilson, absorbed and diluted the Progressive Era's ideals into their own version of progressivism mixed with white supremacy—they softened capitalism, but not for everybody, and not enough to change the basis of the economy in finance capitalism and exploitation.

Indeed, the movements to secure protection from capitalism's worst predations would more and more find legitimacy and power through exclusion of Black citizens. Put another way: the wages of whiteness continued to serve as a political tool, impeding class solidarity and revolution.

The Populist Party's failure to unite poor farmers across racial lines meant its goals were co-opted by Southern Democrats. While some progressive and populist groups resisted white supremacy and Black laborers joined progressive coalitions, mainstream progressivism at the ballot box became intertwined with racial exclusion. This era saw peak state-sanctioned violence by groups like the Ku Klux Klan and Northern unions. The "people's movement" simultaneously fought corporate monopolies while suppressing Black workers, narrowing the definition of "the people" to white men.

WOODROW WILSON, REGARDED AS the intellectual father of progressive policymaking, embodied both the achievements and the contradictions of progressivism. Political scientists Jacob Hacker and Paul Pierson note that Wilson sought to build a mixed economy, a vision that Roosevelt's New Deal would later expand. Wilson presided over the Gilded Age, when industrial titans—men like Carnegie, Rockefeller, Morgan, and Cornelius Vanderbilt, the archetypal robber barons— accumulated unprecedented private wealth and influence. Progressives, wary of the monopolistic power of trusts, focused on breaking up corporate domination, particularly in banking and finance. Wilson decried the concentration of economic power, famously stating, "Our system of credit is privately concentrated. . . . The growth of the nation . . . is in the hands of a few men." His administration created the Federal Reserve to counterbalance this concentration, establishing a public central bank accountable to the people.

But while Wilson expanded the federal government's role in curbing corporate power, he faced resistance from the Supreme Court, whose pro-business rulings defined the "*Lochner* era." In *Lochner v. New York*, the court prioritized property rights over worker protections, deeming laws that limited work hours unconstitutional under the Fourteenth Amendment—a Reconstruction-era amendment intended to protect freed slaves. Ironically, this amendment was more often invoked to protect corporate interests than the rights of Black Americans, who continued to face disenfranchisement, lynching, and systemic exclusion from due process.

Wilson's presidency also witnessed violent clashes between labor and industry, including the 1914 Ludlow Massacre, where a private militia killed striking miners and their families. The event was a turning point, prompting Wilson to send federal troops to de-escalate the conflict and leading to greater federal support for unions. Wilson championed child labor protections and antitrust legislation, including the Clayton Antitrust Act of 1914, which strengthened efforts to break up monopolies. His administration also introduced progressive taxation and created the Federal Trade Commission to oversee antitrust enforcement independent of Congress and the executive branch.

Despite his progressive economic reforms, Wilson institutionalized white supremacy in the federal government. He segregated federal offices, prohibited the hiring of Black employees, and purged those appointed by his predecessors. Wilson's administration reflected the broader Southern Democratic agenda, which combined progressive economic policies with a commitment to racial hierarchy. Southern legislators resisted free markets, sought credit reforms to benefit white farmers, and excluded Black farmers from federal programs like the Federal Farm Loan Act of 1916, which was administered locally to ensure racial discrimination.

Wilson's progressivism was also steeped in the pseudoscience of racial eugenics, which framed societal reforms as tools to preserve racial hierarchies. Eugenics, widely accepted by scientists and reformers of the era, sought to justify racial segregation and the exclusion of non-white populations under the guise of scientific advancement. Phrenology and social Darwinism depicted Black Americans as inferior, rationalizing their economic and social subjugation. In the media and in the academy, Black Americans were popularly portrayed as unevolved primates or gorillas dressed as humans. The dominant stereotype of them was as "subhuman or a beast." Columbia University professor Howard Odum approvingly quoted a physician who'd concluded that Black people were "as destitute of morals as any of the lower animals." Dr. E. C. Ferguson explained to the medical association of Georgia that the "negro is monkey-like; has no sympathy for his fellowman; has no regard for the truth, and when the truth would answer his purpose the best, he will lie. He is without gratitude or appreciation of anything done to him; is a natural born thief,—will steal anything, no matter how worthless. He has no morals."

Northern segregation codes were reinforced, and Jim Crow laws lived to reproduce injustice for another half century—all on account of the misconstrued "facts" of human evolution. In his 1909 paper "Evolution of the Race Problem," Du Bois lamented the scientific community's embrace of race science, which he called a misuse of Darwin's "splendid scientific work" put in service of a "justification of disfranchisement, the personal humiliation of Jim-Crowism, a curtailed and purposely limited system of education and a virtual acknowledgment of the inevitable and universal inferiority of black men." He called this perversion of science to prop up oppression "the most cowardly dilemma that a strong people ever thrust upon the weak." Du Bois saw in Darwin's ideas a capacious view of humanity's potential: "Freedom has come to mean not individual caprice or aberration but social self-realization in an endless chain of selves, and freedom for such development is not the denial but the central assertion of the evolutionary theory. So, too, the doctrine of human equality passes through the fire of scientific inquiry not obliterated but transfigured." Rather than promoting possibility and freedom, however, the social Darwinists reduced evolutionary theory to yet another justification for political power premised on white racial superiority.

This is the underbelly of the Progressive Era, and understanding the link between progressive reform and race science is crucial to understanding the progressive mixed-state project. This "scientific" theory of white supremacy was swiftly dropped by American scientists as soon as it was picked up and acted on by the Nazis.

Once Black people were relegated to subhuman status, however, it became justifiable to subjugate them economically. This ideology also fueled the criminalization of Blackness. If the essential nature of some races was subversiveness and criminality, the logical response was heavy policing. The Irish and Italians were also deemed "criminal races," but no races or nationalities were as strongly subjected to a coercive and systematic police state as Black men. The entire structure of American policing began in the post-Reconstruction South as a means to tyrannize and subjugate them. As Khalil Gibran Muhammad explains, "For white Americans of every ideological stripe—from radical southern racists to northern progressives—African American criminality became one of the most widely accepted bases for justifying prejudicial thinking, discriminatory treatment, and/or acceptance of racial violence as an instrument of public safety."

Not only did the nation's scientific community aid in the project of racial hierarchy; historians concocted a narrative of the Civil War as a tale of heroic battle by victimized Southern patriots against Black aggression and violence. Thomas Dixon's 1905 novel and play *The Clansmen* reinforced this Southern fairy tale. Credited with reviving the Klan to its most violent apex in the 1920s, the novel was adapted by D. W. Griffith into a blockbuster film, *The Birth of a Nation*, a technically innovative, full-length silent movie, and the first film to be screened in the White House, by private invitation of President Wilson. The film and the history mended the breach between North and South at the sacrifice of Black freedom.

The Progressive Era's legacy is a paradox. While it laid the groundwork for reforms that expanded the role of government in protecting citizens and regulating the economy, it did so by reinforcing systemic racism. Progressivism defined "the people" narrowly, excluding nonwhite Americans and perpetuating structures of inequality. This duality reveals a system so deeply infected by racism that even its attempts at reform entrenched racial hierarchy. And reforms rooted in exclusionary compromises are ultimately unsustainable.

CHAPTER 3

The Catch-22 of Black Banks

THE FLAGRANT RACISM THAT NOURISHED this racial order, by now marrow-deep in the white South, triggered a mass exodus from the only home, inhospitable as it was, that Black Southerners had ever known. Between 1910 and 1970, the Great Migration saw approximately six million Black Americans flee the South, fundamentally altering the demographic fabric of the country. Where the South was plagued with racial injustice and no perceivable economic opportunity, the North held the promise of better jobs for more just compensation. In his poem "The South," Langston Hughes wrote of "The lazy, laughing South / With blood on its mouth" and "The cold-faced North," calling the latter "a kinder mistress" that beckoned Black people fleeing inhospitable conditions below the Mason-Dixon Line to a brighter reality above it.

The North did indeed welcome Black migrants, as well as immigrants from across the world, by segregating them into racial ghettos and putting them to work for low wages in the booming industrial sector. E. Franklin Frazier called this kinder mistress and her ghettos the "cities of destruction." For while the Black community could leave behind the Southern plantation and Jim Crow, the poverty, discrimination, and violence of American racism could not be shaken. Though it took a different shape, white racism was, in many ways, as pervasive in the North as it was in the South. It was racism that spawned Black ghettos and the tightly tangled social, political, and economic tendrils therein.

Black Southerners moving into Northern cities drew out Northern racial hostility, resulting in segregation. With white institutions often closed to Black people during the migration period, many Black banks, savings and loan institutions, and credit unions formed to serve Northern Black communities. Though these institutions benefited from the concentration of Black labor, they also experienced much the same economic stagnation that similar operations in the South had. Many ultimately failed, but some established lasting footholds despite staggering odds.

The Binga State Bank and the Douglass National Bank, dubbed the "titans of Black finance," were both located in Chicago. Jesse Binga found a way to profit off white flight by buying property from whites desperate to sell, then flipping and selling those properties at fair and reasonable rates to Black buyers. Beloved in his community, Binga quickly rose to the top of Black real estate in Chicago and eventually opened the Binga State Bank in 1908. The bank thrived, and so did Binga. His success was met with racially fueled violence; his home, which was in a white neighborhood, was bombed seven times. Each bombing was accompanied by a note urging him to leave, but Binga refused. "I will not run," he maintained. "The race is at stake and not myself. If they can make me move they will have accomplished much of their aim because they can say, 'We made Jesse Binga move; certainly you'll have to move' to all the rest. If they can make the leaders move, what show will the small buyers have?"

BINGA'S BANK WAS LAUDED by both Black and white bankers. He became a paying member of the Chicago Clearinghouse, a co-op for high-powered banks designed to protect one another in case of crisis. But the 1929 stock market crash brought his dreams to a screeching halt and sent the Binga State Bank into a tailspin. Despite the fact that Binga was one of the founding members of the fund, the Chicago Clearinghouse declined his request for a loan. It was reported that the chairman had referred to the institution, which had stood as a beacon of hope for the Black community, as "a little nigger bank that does not mean anything."

If we understand trust to be the basis of sound banking, then racism threatens the very viability of Black banks—the elite members of the Chicago Clearinghouse did not trust Binga's bank (which they used a racial epithet to describe). Racism also had tangible effects on Binga's asset portfolio of mortgages on Black homes, which could not be sold to the market. Binga explained that he had selected the best of his mortgages, and he couldn't sell them, even with a haircut of over 50 percent. Illinois auditors closed Binga's bank on July 31, 1930, and his depositors—many of them once members of the Black elite—lost most of their savings. The Chicago Clearinghouse extended aid to every other member bank, allowing them to survive the Great Depression.

The failure of this bank and the ruination its closure brought to many wealthy Black Americans dealt a hard blow to morale in the Black community. Sadly, Binga's downfall did not end there. He was indicted for embezzlement because of his bank's failure and sent to prison. As far as I can tell, very few bankers (some sources say none) went to prison after the Great Depression. Except for Binga. The state brought criminal penalties against him for violating state banking law. Clarence Darrow, one of the nation's most reputable attorneys, came to his defense, stating during his parole hearing that he had "known Binga for thirty years and he is a man of fine character." But Binga remained in prison for six years, until 1941, when ten thousand Chicago residents signed a petition in support of his parole. Binga's wealth did not lead to political power or equality. The truth was that absolute equality before the law had to come first.

THOUGH NEW YORK CITY was home to a larger population of income-earning Black Americans than Chicago and boasted a more robust Black business sector, there were no Black banks in the Big Apple. Several attempts were made, but none took. There are a few possible reasons why New York City remained a Black bank desert despite ongoing demand, but by far the most likely is that white banks kept Black banks from getting charters. One such white-owned bank was the Chelsea Exchange Bank, which had a monopoly on Harlem depositors. In fact, by 1916, 85 percent of the Chelsea Exchange Bank's depositors were Black individuals and 14 percent were Black businesses. Still, the Chelsea Exchange Bank had not a single Black board member. It did not make loans to Harlem, either—it just took the deposits of the neighborhood's Black residents. In response to accusations about its refusal to extend loans to Black people, the bank claimed that its policy was to deny such requests "unless the applicant can show a satisfactory balance and business statement and has a generally good character."

The Chelsea Exchange Bank's inequitable practices were symptomatic of growing racist notions that Black people, unlike other immigrants, were inherently incapable of success in business. One white teller of the Chelsea Exchange Bank justified the gross imbalance he witnessed while working there, explaining that white loans were safer than Black loans because "the Negro is entirely untutored in the business world; he is historically not a business man." Of course, such attitudes only lengthened and steepened the economic uphill battle for Black people. As George Bernard Shaw put it, "the haughty American nation . . . makes the Negro clean its boots, and then proves the moral and physical inferiority of the Negro by the fact that he is a shoeblack."

IT WAS IN THIS time of heavy Northern segregation that a vibrant Black community was created and Marcus Garvey rose to prominence, trumpeting Black nationalism with the intent to uplift the "poor Black masses" living in Northern ghettos. He argued for the need to build an entirely independent community—to build the walls erected in the name of Jim Crow even higher and keep the whites out. Garvey, dubbed "the Black Moses," considered Black people to be "a mighty race" and insisted that only two options existed: either they must go back to Africa, or they must reap reparations for slavery from the American government and create a sovereign nation in America. In 1912, Garvey founded the Universal Negro Improvement Association (UNIA) to accomplish his goals for the Black community. His pro-segregation rhetoric inspired an unlikely allyship with the KKK's grand wizard, which alienated him from other Black leaders. To Du Bois, Garvey was "the most dangerous enemy of the Negro race in America."

Though he differed wildly from many influential Black leaders with regard to his political and social vision for Black America, Garvey's economic vision neatly paralleled Booker T. Washington's. He was an advocate for capitalism, urging Black Harlem to "be not deceived, wealth is strength, wealth is power, wealth is influence, wealth is justice, is liberty, is real human rights." He launched his own enterprises centered on segregation and published early voices of the Harlem Renaissance in his newspaper, *The Negro World*. Ultimately, though, he was deported to Jamaica after being arrested for mail fraud, which many considered to be a trumped-up charge by the federal government against a perceived political agitator.

Garvey's personal trajectory as a Black American leader ended in failure, but his legacy would remain. Raised by two Garvey disciples that took issue with Black aspirations for integration into a society that continued to reject them, Malcolm X took up pieces of Garvey's mantle. So, too, would a number of Black radical groups, including the Black Panthers, the Nation of Islam, and the Rastas.

Black nationalism took root most readily in Black Northern ghettos, where residents noted the predominance of white-owned businesses with anger. The movement pushed for a completely parallel and rival Black economy.

Richard R. Wright Sr., who was born enslaved in Georgia and helped his family get on its feet after slavery ended, saw Black banking as "a tangible start toward real financial emancipation." He founded the National Negro Bankers Association (NNBA) in 1927 with the goal of uniting Black banks to increase resilience and stability. Unfortunately, the Black population was reluctant to trust that Black banks were as safe and reliable as white banks. The memory of the tragic failure and loss of savings in the Freedman's Savings Bank collapse still lingered in the community, inhibiting trust in banking in general. In the days before the federal government guaranteed bank deposits, successful banking was impossible without trust. Seeing that the Black press readily published news of Black bank failures, the NNBA implored

Black publications such as the *Pittsburgh Courier*, the *Norfolk Journal and Guide*, and the *Philadelphia Tribune* to do their part in eradicating these fears. But this job proved more difficult than the NNBA had anticipated. Decades of racist rhetoric had sent stems out into every sector of American society. Even in the Black community itself, the seeds of internalized racism had begun to germinate.

Though he did not extend assistance to individual Black banks, in 1927 President Coolidge did set up the Commerce Department's Division of Negro Affairs, which supported Black businesses. The department was largely toothless, though, and did little but spread information. The NNBA was just starting to find its sea legs when the Great Depression ravaged the Black banking industry. Even Maggie Walker, who rightly pointed out that "a thousand times more Negro money is lost year after year in other banks than is lost in Negro banks," could not undo the damage. The reality was that even without a depression, Black banks had not been able to accrue enough capital in the segregated economy to stay afloat when the economic tide went out.

WITHOUT A THRIVING BLACK business sector in which to invest, Black bank loans were almost solely used for residential real estate. Predictably, white banks rarely—if ever—lent to prospective Black homeowners. And these loans were extremely risky, since property values plummeted in areas with Black homeownership. On the heels of the 1910 migration, stringent segregation in the North was rigorously enforced with violence, zoning laws, and racial agreements, giving Black people no choice but to stay in the ghettos. Racial violence frequently erupted at the seams between Black ghettos and white neighborhoods.

Only about 2 percent of the Northern Black population—the Black upper class—could afford to buy homes with the commonly requisite 50 percent down payment. Those who could, like Jesse Binga, were regularly targeted by angry whites. These instances of violence stemmed from fears that the ghetto was encroaching on white territory. Indeed, once a neighborhood "tipped" into being perceived as a "Black neighborhood," whites left in droves. Devoid of residents privileged by the support of the state, these neighborhoods would indeed decline, eventually folding into the adjacent ghetto landscape. A member of the Black middle class who broke the color barrier and purchased a home in a white neighborhood would pay the high white-neighborhood price; then, precisely because of their purchase, their new property would plummet in value. Not only did Black homeowners pay an exorbitant financial cost just to occupy their homes; they paid an even greater psychological cost, for they could expect threats of violence or actual violence by angry mobs of white neighbors. This phenomenon was yet another cruel paradox keeping the economic color line intact.

Although practically every group of immigrants that flocked to the North in the early 1900s experienced racism from established populations, no other racial or ethnic groups were subject to the same decline in property value. In fact, given the deeply embedded racism in the American economy after decades of ideological warfare, a neighborhood's home values were derived precisely from their proximity to Black people. Homogenous white neighborhoods were the most expensive, with mixed white immigrant neighborhoods next, on down to the Black ghetto, which defined the very bottom in terms of property values.

Systemic racism works by combining the ideologies of racial superiority with the means of acquiring wealth. If a home owned by a Black family automatically declined in value because it was a

Black family's home, how would Black families ever build equity? Put another way, whiteness became synonymous with wealth, and Blackness with the lack of it. The trick is that only a minority of white people could attain wealth or homeownership at the time— the rest received the "wages of whiteness," per the system of white supremacy that supplanted class solidarity. The wages of whiteness meant that poor whites would perpetually associate themselves with the wealthiest in the society and view Black people as the greatest threat to their security. Mobs of poor white immigrants challenged every new Black homeowner because their entrance to the neighborhood meant plummeting home values for the other precarious homeowners.

The vicious cycle meant that Black neighborhoods would always be in a state of decline. On the flip side of that coin, property value in all-white neighborhoods continued to increase. The ghetto rental market experienced gross inflation, as high demand in these already-dense areas caused rent to climb more than 50 precent higher than rent elsewhere. Segregation punctured holes at all points along the Black wealth continuum—banking, business, real estate, savings—draining money at an alarming rate.

The aftershock of these massively imbalanced circumstances during the Great Depression rattled the Black banking sector, too. Housing loans immediately went underwater, there was no ready market for Black mortgages, banks were unable to lend at a profit, and assets were simply not appreciating in value. The hope was that either Black communities would be able to buy enough property to stabilize housing prices or whites would stop evacuating neighborhoods where Black people purchased property, but this hope did not bear fruit. A positive feedback loop for white wealth entwined with a negative feedback loop for Black poverty. Segregation remained rigidly rooted, and racism sank deeper into the soil. Even in the Roaring Twenties, while the stock market soared and American fortunes climbed to unprecedented levels, the Black community remained mired in deep poverty because of the entrenched ideologies of racism, made manifest in segregation patterns and home values. Having not ridden the bull market, Black communities found the bear market even more painful. The adage went that when Wall Street got a cold, Harlem got pneumonia. And the crash of 1929 was much more than a cold.

During the Great Depression, when the country's economic system broadly faced hardship, Jim Crow segregation acted as a magnifying lens on Black poverty. Disease, starvation, and infant mortality rates were staggeringly higher in the Black community. In his book *An American Dilemma*, Gunnar Myrdal provided this startling analysis of the situation at hand:

> Except for a small minority enjoying upper or middle class status, the masses of American Negroes, in the rural South and in the segregated slum quarters in Southern and Northern cities, are destitute. They own little property; even their household goods are mostly inadequate and dilapidated. Their incomes are not only low but irregular. They thus live from day to day and have scant security for the future.

As Myrdal correctly deduced, America's pretense of justice, equality, and freedom for all lay sharply at odds with the overt injustice, inequality, and oppression experienced by its Black citizens. In the South, racial violence and hostility raged unabated. Lynchings were frequent and flagrantly ignored by the law, education was poor or entirely absent for Black children, and Black Americans continued to lose land. Due to these impossible conditions, more were forced to migrate North, causing the ghettos to further swell and stagnate.

Against these conditions, Du Bois began to sound a bit like his rival, Washington, in advocating for Black people to practice "voluntary and increased segregation" and to bolster and build upon their community "by careful autonomy and planned economic organization." Unlike Washington, though, Du Bois remained deeply wary of Black capitalism, warning Black businessmen to pursue economic health for the Black community at large rather than for themselves as individuals. In *The Mis-education of the Negro*, Dr. Carter G. Woodson attributed the failures of Black banking to internalized racism instilled by white hegemony; if there was robust community support for Black banks, he argued, they would be much more stable and successful.

Abram Harris, the first nationally renowned Black economist, had Marxist roots and was critical of the trajectory Black capitalism seemed to be taking. In his book *The Negro as Capitalist*, Harris accused Black bankers of benefitting from "skillful exploitation of the Negro masses." He criticized them for enriching themselves and the Black elite at the expense of poor Black people. Yet the main thesis of that book—one he proved by a thorough analysis of the balance sheets of the most successful Black banks of the era—was that Black banks could never achieve their intended aim insofar as the forces of segregation acted as a depressive force on Black property values. Black banks were not only powerless to keep Black money inside the artificial barriers of the Black ghetto, but hastened the outflow of funds from the community. Black banks could take deposits from Black customers and lend to Black home buyers, but each time they lent money to a Black borrower to purchase a home, the funds would

immediately leave the community because the homes were all purchased from white sellers. And because white-owned banks were not
lending to the Black community, it was a one-way funnel of money
out. Black banks operated within a system of white-owned property
that they were powerless to change, despite their efforts.

Further, Black banks had three primary disadvantages: poverty
among depositors, housing segregation, and a fractured economic system that prevented money from circulating effectively within Black
communities. Black depositors, largely low-income workers, made
small and unstable deposits. These deposits were costly for banks, as
servicing small accounts demanded resources comparable to those
devoted to larger accounts without yielding proportional profits. To
manage risk, Black banks held higher reserves and capital ratios than
white banks, reducing their ability to issue profitable loans through
fractional reserve lending. (Fractional reserve lending allows banks to
multiply money by issuing loans, which creates new deposits in the
banking system. For example, if $100 is deposited in Bank A and 90
percent is lent to a borrower, the borrower's loan becomes a new deposit
in Bank B. This process expands the money supply.) This practice con-
strained their capacity to multiply wealth, leaving them less profitable
and less impactful within their communities.

Segregation reinforced a feedback loop that disadvantaged Black
banks and communities. While white banks retained wealth and
multiplied capital, Black banks' assets depreciated, and their liabili-
ties remained costly. Despite efforts by leaders like Du Bois to build
a self-sustaining Black economy, the structural inequities of property
ownership and segregation made this goal unattainable. The Great
Depression exacerbated these problems, deepening poverty and under-
mining hopes of economic progress. The very mechanisms of bank-

ing that created wealth for white communities worked against Black banks, leaving them unable to generate or retain capital. This structural imbalance highlights the enduring challenges of segregation and systemic racism in wealth creation.

Disagreements between Black leaders aside, the bottom line remained that Jim Crow gave Black Americans pathetically few options. The system was so intricately rigged against them in so many ways that, as Du Bois put it, a prosperous future seemed "a hope not hopeless but unhopeful." Activists continued to push for civil rights and integration, but the fight had yet to yield victories, large or small. Dim as it seemed at times, though, hope for change remained alive. And change, in fact, was on the horizon.

CHAPTER 4

The New Deal for White America

■   ■   ■   ■   ■   ■   ■

Between 1934 and 1968, the federal government funded and insured the entire credit and banking system. New home construction nearly doubled from 1936 to 1941. In 1936, the FHA had lent half a billion dollars in guaranteed mortgages. By 1939, it had issued $4 billion in mortgages and home improvement loans. Housing starts were 332,000 in 1936 and 619,000 in 1941. The New Deal mortgage loan programs created the thirty-year fixed-rate mortgage, backed it up with the force of the U.S. Treasury, and developed a mortgage market unlike anything the world had ever seen. The government lending programs administered by the new credit and banking agencies included the Home Owners' Loan Corporation (HOLC), the Federal Home Loan Bank system (FHLB), the Federal Farm Loan Act (FFLA), and the Federal Housing Administration (FHA). These were all geared toward the rapid and effective dissemination of low-cost credit to new homeowners. Coupled with postwar economic growth, they fostered a robust home-owning, capital-creating, and predominantly white middle class. The FHA did not lend money itself, but it established a large insurance fund backed by the U.S. Treasury that would guarantee all approved mortgage loans, which shifted the bulk of the risk of loan default from banks to the government. The FHA also produced protocol and standards on all loans.

Not only did the billions in mortgage loans create the equity-owning American middle class; they enriched investors by enabling a secondary market with the implementation of government-sponsored enterprises (GSEs) through the 1938 introduction of the Federal National Mortgage Association (FNMA, or "Fannie Mae") and the Government National Mortgage Association (GNMA, or Ginnie Mae). These GSEs fostered a secondary market for private and institutional investors in one part of the country to invest in mortgages in another, ensuring that capital would always find yield. The government created the platform, or "market," that drew in capital from all corners and multiplied it.

The New Deal's "deal" with banks was akin to a social contract: the state subsidized banks with deposit insurance and a whole host of public guarantees and direct capital infusions, which the banks could distribute to their customers at a profit. In return, federal regulators imposed restrictions on what they could do (only deposit taking and lending), where they could operate (only within a particular community or region), and even what kind of spread they could make (3 percent on deposits, 6 percent on loans). Regulation Q, passed under the Glass-Steagall Act, capped the amount of interest paid on deposits to prohibit bank competition. For a while, the only competition allowed between banks was who could give away the best toaster!

Private banking was a myth. A bank charter allowed a bank to use public funds to make private profits. Between 1933 and the 1970s, hundreds of thousands of small community banks, credit unions, and thrifts were formed—and they were safe, stable, and profitable. This

was the heyday of American banking. Never had banks been so numerous, safe, and profitable. For example, between 1934 and 1980, there
were 23,564 new charters for credit unions. Total commercial bank
branches grew from around 3,000 in 1935 to 40,000 in 1980. Some
11,000 S&Ls were created in the 1930s, with many more added over
the years. This period coincided with a booming banking sector, no
banking crises, unprecedented national and individual wealth, and a
complete restoration of public confidence in the sector.

The dark underbelly of the system was that it wasn't available
to non-white Americans. Not just by accident, but by design. Black
homeowners and Black neighborhoods would not be insured by government programs. Lawyers and courts ensured racial "homogeneity"
by including "racial covenants" in each deed, prohibiting the home's
sale to "anyone not of the Caucasian race." The golden era was a manufactured prosperity that left out Black communities entirely. It was
achieved at their expense.

In his first inaugural address, Roosevelt claimed that no less than
the "future of *essential democracy*" depended on getting these reforms
right. The New Deal responded with a Keynesian program that was
as close to state planning or democratic socialism as the United States
has ever come. Afterward, with businesses and banks booming, economists began telling stories about the triumphs of the free market. That
wasn't the only irony. From Jefferson to Wilson, from the Constitution
to the New Deal, progressive reformists fought big-money power for
the sake of the people.

And all the while, their reforms were built on a bedrock of white
supremacy. It was the Southern Democrats in the Senate who pushed
through FDR's New Deal—the same bloc that made sure no anti-
lynching bill reached the floor, despite 240 attempts. FDR's electoral

coalition was larger than the South, but the Senate was designed, even at its founding, to give the South a check on popular democracy. The Southern senators headed up all the key committees because their electoral monopoly—thanks to voter-suppression laws—meant they were primary-proof and thus could achieve seniority, the currency of power in the Senate. The Senate was both the reactionary and regressive force blocking civil rights for a generation and the force that turned the New Deal into a massive subsidy for white Americans—in order to maintain the sacrosanct racial order of the South. The Democrats controlled the South, the Southern bloc controlled the Senate, the Senate controlled the passage of laws, and the South itself was controlled by Jim Crow. Southern senators, for example, ensured that domestic workers were exempt from Social Security protection and that farm loans would be controlled by local rather than national offices.

The New Deal built the lily-white suburb of homeowners and the segregated Black ghetto through redlining. Again, in order to pass the progressive legislation, Roosevelt was left with little choice but to capitulate to Southern Democrats in the Senate, who staunchly and cohesively demanded that their economic structure—and the racial hierarchy that supported it—remain intact. This meant categorically excluding Black people from significant government endowments, resulting in laws that could easily be described as "white affirmative action." The Senate Southern Democrats were a mighty minority, and Roosevelt understood his devil's bargain: sweeping social reform or equitable treatment of the races. His choice—the former—would have implications for generations to come.

Though the letter of the New Deal did not make explicit mention of race, the suite of laws carefully carved Black Americans out of the newly woven social safety net. In many cases, before New Deal bills were even sent to a vote, Southern senators finagled the language to keep Black people from receiving aid. In other instances, legislators overtly campaigned to keep Black workers on their low social and economic rung. Florida Representative James Mark Wilcox candidly explained this reasoning: "There is another matter of great importance in the South and that is the problem of our Negro labor. There has always been a difference in the wage scale of white and colored labor. . . . [Fixing wages] might work on some sections of the United States but those of us who know the true situation know that it just will not work in the South. You cannot put the Negro and the white man on the same basis and get away with it." In cases where Black people were not excluded from the letter of the law, the Southern bloc sought to fill local administrative positions with people guaranteed to reinforce the racial order. Slowly but effectively, the New Deal became "a sieve with holes just big enough for the majority of Negroes to fall through."

Many of the exclusions were achieved by wording legislation to favor labor commonly done by whites. Another by-product of this cruel sleight of hand was that labor-protecting exclusions—particularly the right to collective action—made it impossible for Black laborers to organize for improved working conditions. While Black workers continued on in unprotected industries, the union movement rapidly gained momentum for white laborers.

If the New Deal was richly imbued with Southern racial regressivism, so too was it steeped in Southern populism, progressivism, and the rejection of unfettered capitalism. Indeed, New Deal America, with its centrally controlled economic planning, Keynesian stimulus programs, and robust social welfare—to say nothing of the restructuring of financial markets to dissolve monopolies, loosen credit, and regulate financial markets—seemed to be inching toward democratic socialism.

THOUGH ROOSEVELT WAS HAMSTRUNG by the Southern Demo-
crats, he did have opportunities to improve the lives of the urban poor.
The Public Works Administration (PWA), one of the largest New Deal
projects, boasted a $6 billion budget. It was run by Secretary of the Inte-
rior Harold Ickes, who had been the president of Chicago's NAACP
chapter. Determined to use the stimulus money to address the increasingly dire conditions in urban slums, Ickes set aside $485 million for
slum rehabilitation. This plan was met with immediate and fierce resistance, as critics argued that it was not the federal government's responsibility to ameliorate housing problems. Without Roosevelt's support,
Ickes's plan was thwarted, and the ghettos slid further into disrepair.

PWA grants were extended, however, for the construction of
bridges and route roads over and through the ghetto. This type of
infrastructure dramatically improved the lives of suburban car com-
muters, diminished public transportation, and—like the freeway
through Durham, North Carolina's Hayti—opened literal rifts in
long-standing urban communities. Government money flowed into
the white middle class in the form of mortgage assistance, allowing
white families to escape the deteriorating cities where the Black poor
remained trapped.

American homeownership was well on its way to becoming one of
the most insidious agents in the widening of the racial wealth gap. The
Home Owners' Loan Corporation (HOLC) simplified and stream-
lined the home mortgage system by initiating standardized home
appraisals. These appraisals used census data and questionnaires to
determine whether or not properties would appreciate in value. The
HOLC then applied this data to maps, where four colors designated
different levels of perceived risk. The most desirable and least risky

areas were green, followed in preference by blue, then yellow. The risk-iest areas were mapped in red. Unfortunately, but unsurprisingly, the green areas were almost exclusively homogeneously white and the red areas were predominately Black. "Redlining," as this practice came to be known, was a self-fulfilling prophecy: neighborhoods labeled red (using race as a proxy for risk level, of course) lost value by virtue of being so labeled, and thus became increasingly less desirable, whereas those marked green grew in desirability.

Redlining was instrumental in cleaving a chasm in the credit market—a chasm that opened precisely along the color line. First, banks used HOLC maps to determine where they would lend. Then the Federal Housing Administration (FHA) and the Veterans Admin-istration (VA) implemented these maps in their mortgage programs, with massive repercussions. For banks, the ideal borrower came to be defined by standards and protocols set by these mortgage-insuring government agencies. Predictably, this ideal borrower was white, male, and middle-class.

It is important to note, though, that the American middle class swelled during this period precisely *because* of these mortgage pro-grams. Many white blue-collar workers reaped the benefits of easier access to home loans, moving from cramped and expensive cities to spacious, mass-produced homes in newly minted suburbs, where they were able to save money and build wealth.

AMERICAN CULTURE UNDERWENT A radical shift during this era, as prefab communities outside cities cropped up, complete with parks, bowling alleys, movie theaters, and neatly manicured lawns. This time period is looked upon wistfully—lionized for its emphasis on family and community as well as its seemingly boundless optimism and prosperity. But the families and communities of Black America were left out of this picturesque vision.

FHA guidelines pointedly and unapologetically enforced segregation, keeping Black people penned up in slums while simultaneously helping whites ascend to the suburbs. The FHA's *Underwriting Manual* explicitly prohibited lending in neighborhoods that were experiencing a change in racial composition, so as to avoid "inharmonious racial groups." The manual stated that it was "necessary that properties shall continue to be occupied by the same social and racial classes," going so far as to suggest "[race-based] subdivision regulations and suitable restrictive covenants." Such racial covenants were upheld until 1950; homeowners kept promises to not sell or rent to non-whites. Other, even more radical measures were taken to enforce the color line—in one case, a white developer in Detroit erected a concrete wall at the seam where a white neighborhood met a Black one to ensure mortgage approval. These tactics, violence against Black homeowners, and FHA policy had the desired result: by 1968, white Americans were the recipients of 98 percent of all FHA loans.

As white middle-class homeowners grew wealthier in their suburbs and urban renters confined to the ghettos sank further into destitution, the opportunity divide between the two yawned wide. In accordance with the American tax system, which ceded educational funding to local governments, tax dollars flowed back into suburban municipalities, allowing for better schools and tighter infrastructure. City poverty, on the other hand, begot crumbling institutions, which begot deeper levels of poverty.

To Americans basking in the benefits of postwar abundance, these very real barriers to Black advancement were invisible. The issues that increasingly plagued Black neighborhoods—among them crime, drug addiction, overpopulation, and disease—were attributed by many a privileged observer to failings of the culture. The cities were disintegrating, and white America pointed a finger at the breakdown of the Black family or low-quality education. These theories, though grossly misguided and willfully ignorant of the very system that bred them, would only gain traction in the decades to come.

Predatory lenders and contract sellers descended on the vulnerable Black population, passing off contractual arrangements as mortgages. Banks that would not lend to prospective Black buyers readily extended loans to speculators so they could snap up properties in the ghetto and "sell" them to Black buyers on contract. Black people were paying exorbitantly more than the rest of the country for rent-to-own property, clinging to a smoke-and-mirrors promise of homeownership in the distant future. But one missed payment would result in a total loss. While the burgeoning white middle class was kept insulated from mortgage market risk by the government, the Black poor were experiencing the full, malignant force of free-market capitalism.

On top of the FHA mortgage loans, a dual market in consumer credit was created during this time. The FHA also had a consumer loan guarantee—short-lived, but around long enough to create a secondary market in consumer credit. In the suburbs, department stores began offering credit cards with a revolving credit line. This type of credit was flexible and low-interest. Once members of the white middle class had settled into homeownership, their appetite for spending grew. The FHA swooped in, bestowing the ability to profit from consumer loans on banks and credit card companies. In response, suburban America thrummed with consumerism. "Revolving credit," which was less costly and fixed than installment lending, became the common practice, greatly expanding purchasing power for borrowers. A credit card, for example, enabled families to make credit purchases of appliances, cars, and furniture—and thanks to government subsidies and interest rate caps, the interest never exceeded 6 percent. But most credit cards, by their terms, were available only to white families. Not only did this new consumer credit system enhance the quality of life for middle-class families; it also afforded them protection against the unexpected but inevitable hazards of life, such as temporary unemployment or a workplace injury. Meanwhile, the very wealthy opted out of the consumer credit market entirely, as they did not need it for comfort or security.

Poor Black Americans were kept out by racism and risk aversion in the finance industry. In the Black ghetto, there was only installment credit for most necessities, including medical care. The way these contracts were structured was that the goods purchased were bundled together, and each payment went to a slice of the total interest and principal. If a few payments were missed, the borrower was deemed to be in default for the entire bundle of goods. Default involved repo men, criminal penalties, and sometimes threats of bodily injury. Far different from revolving credit cards. Because of the high costs of credit, ghetto residents found themselves paying three to five times more for lower-quality goods and services.

BEFORE THERE WAS A Montgomery bus boycott, there were boycotts and protests of these installment credit arrangements. In Harlem, boycotts were blessed by the courts as a free speech right, and a few community groups teamed up with state legislatures to begin the process of reforms. The leaders of the Civil Rights Movement—integrationists and nationalists—saw economic rights as going hand in hand with civil rights. The establishment of several Black banks became vehicles for boycott and protest.

But a self-perpetuating debt cycle awaited those who managed to claw their way into the small Black middle class. Black families in the suburbs accrued debt rapidly, as they were forced to borrow for necessities like cars and appliances. Higher levels of debt meant higher interest rates, and higher interest rates kept middle-class Black residents from accruing wealth at anywhere near the same rate as their white counterparts. The unfortunate by-product of this vicious cycle was that white families came to hold eight times as much wealth as Black families—the average wealth of white families was $76,000 in today's dollars, compared with $9,000 for average Black families. This wealth gap persisted from the 1930s to the 1960s, an era otherwise touted by economists as "the great leveling"; the general wealth gap between the rich and poor was at a historic low, thanks to all the New Deal subsidies to the middle class and high income taxes for the wealthy. This was a time when the American economy became the strongest in the world. Yet this abundance was built on explicit racial exclusions that prevented most Black families from enjoying the spoils.

The injustice of the wildly unbalanced Jim Crow credit market was painfully apparent to the Black community, and the need to provide their own mortgages was equally clear. Chicago native Dempsey J. Travis stepped up to the task. In 1953, bent on lifting "the 'cotton curtain' between the black community and the FHA," he founded Sivart Mortgage Corporation, which sought to reclaim the large percentage of Black savings held in white institutions. The FHA finally approved his application for accreditation in 1961, after denying it six times. Finding a bank that would offer him enough capital to pursue his aims was tricky. Despite being backed by the FHA, Travis found his loan requests refused again and again, and he was met with condescension at every turn. "The cost of maintaining black pride and personal dignity," he noted, "can be extremely high." At last, he managed to secure a $200,000 line of credit to fund his operation.

For Travis, his work as a Black businessman was inextricably tied to his work as a Black activist. Though his endeavors looked a lot like Booker T. Washington's rhetoric made manifest, he drew his inspiration from Marcus Garvey's emphasis on building the Black community from within. He also resisted, like Garvey, the push to fully integrate into white America. At the end of his career, Travis came to believe that government assistance would be necessary for Black people to achieve equality.

The Carver Federal Savings Bank in Harlem, which would become the largest Black-owned financial institution in the country, was run by another man who considered his work to involve equal parts business savvy and activism. Reverend Milton Moran Weston II was a priest and a civil rights activist as well as a banker. He saw the "flagrant ignorance" and racism with which white bankers treated Black customers and decided to help the community himself, observing that "the resurrection of the community has to start with housing. When you have good housing, then it's possible to move on to a stable family life." In addition to his tireless work as a preacher and a key figure in Black business, Weston organized for labor rights and collective action. When he retired in 1997, he had served the Carver bank for nearly fifty years.

ANOTHER STRONG PROPONENT OF Black banking was none other than Martin Luther King Jr. Indeed, vociferous support of Black enterprise was one of the most consistent components of his revolutionary leadership. Better known for his "I Have a Dream" speech's rhetoric of desegregation, King's support for Black-exclusive banking was a natural companion to his strategy of boycotting white institutions. King drafted the ambitious blueprint of his movement in a piece entitled "We Are Still Walking," illustrating his agenda as "a long-range constructive program" including the establishment of a Black-owned bank in Montgomery and the organization of a credit union.

Some Black bankers were hesitant to align themselves outright with the growing movement of boycotts and marches. A. G. Gaston, the founder of Birmingham's Citizens Federal Savings and Loan Association, aligned himself with Washington's philosophy for Black advancement. He felt King's leadership was too radical and lamented that it did not leave room for compromise with white leaders. Gaston thought the Civil Rights Movement should focus on evening the economic playing field, an outcome that would be achieved through hard work and negotiation, not through sit-ins and other such inflammatory acts of defiance. Nevertheless, he extended financial support to the movement—even to King himself.

Other prominent Black figures, like the socialist intellectual E. Franklin Frazier, were deeply critical of Black businessmen and other members of the Black elite. Frazier referred to Washington's promised land, in which Black people were finally considered equals due to their hard work, thrift, and financial success, as "a world of make-believe." He levered his most scathing critiques, though, at the Black bourgeoisie, whom he referred to as "house slaves," culpable in the exploitation of the rest of the Black community (or, as he put it, the "field slaves"). Malcolm X and other Black radical leaders would carry this class tension forward through the Civil Rights Movement. Though his accusations were not entirely baseless, Frazier failed to see the bottom line: Black bankers and businessmen were also dramatically hindered by the Jim Crow credit market.

Between the New Deal era and the civil rights era, the Black banking bloc struggled to survive, let alone prosper, while the broader American banking system grew and thrived. This paradigm was far from accidental—in fact, it was a direct result of targeted efforts implemented and enforced by the FHA to curtail Black mortgage lending and facilitate white mortgage lending.

Thanks to the FHA and its flexible notions of "whiteness," the ghettos that trapped America's other immigrant groups did eventually improve themselves out of existence—Italian, Irish, German, Polish, and Jewish immigrants, once derided as subhuman, were considered Caucasian enough to qualify for an FHA mortgage. Indeed, a contrast with the viable banks created by Italian, Jewish, German, Irish, and Asian immigrants highlights the dilemma faced by Black banks. Each of these immigrant groups confronted racial bias and exclusion, but the key difference was that none of them was ever systematically, uniformly, and legally segregated to the extent and for the length of time the Black community was. Many immigrants eventually left their overcrowded ghettos and settled in suburbs from which, through violence, zoning restrictions, or racial covenants, Black people were barred. One clear example of this divergent path is the Bank of Italy, formed in San Francisco to serve Italian immigrants who could not get loans from mainstream banks. Eventually, the Bank of Italy grew and merged into the mainstream U.S. banking system—just as Italian immigrants assimilated into American society. What was formerly the Bank of Italy is now the Bank of America—the largest and one of the most profitable banks in the country.

The success of immigrant banks should not be misinterpreted. It was not self-help and community support that allowed them to finance themselves out of the ghetto. They left the ghetto first. They did so only after being accepted as "white," not through segregating their money.

The bootstraps they were given were government-guaranteed mortgage loans, from which Black people were excluded. Doubtless, many immigrants worked hard to achieve the American dream of homeownership. So, too, did Black people.

THE MYTH OF THE self-made immigrant began during this time, and would soon be sedimented in the American psyche, immortalized in works such as Frank Capra's film *It's a Wonderful Life*, which pulls from Capra's own rags-to-riches immigrant saga and holds self-help community banking up as a shining beacon of hope. But an Italian immigrant like Capra could grab government-provided bootstraps like the GI Bill and the FHA to support him as he rose from slum to suburb. Black Americans received no such boost, and their hard-earned money was bled from them by contract sellers, slumlords, and disproportionately expensive mortgages.

However, the Civil Rights Movement, which was slowly gathering momentum at this time, brought about some change. The first act of mass civil disobedience, a march on Washington in 1941 to protest discrimination in government defense contracts, led a rattled Roosevelt to sign Executive Order 8802, forbidding military contractors from discriminating "because of race, creed, color, or national origin." A. Philip Randolph, who organized the march, compared it to the Emancipation Proclamation. Randolph would go on to help organize the 1963 March on Washington, where he spoke alongside Dr. King.

Fueled by the observation that white businesses were profiting off the ghetto and leaving Black businesses no avenue by which to compete, Black activists—spanning the spectrum from Black nationalists to the conservative National Negro Business League—united to push for "Bigger and Better Negro Business." Another community push for change coalesced around the idea of boycotting white businesses—particularly those that would not hire Black people. The Harlem Labor Union took up this cause, creating the "Don't Buy Where You Can't Work" platform and urging Black leaders across the country to effectively wield their "purchasing power." These efforts would become integral to the larger Civil Rights Movement, which was just cresting the horizon.

After World War II, Black veterans, who had put their lives on the line for America, rightly began clamoring for better treatment. Americans were once again faced with a paradox: How could they continue to justify racial injustice at home when the whole world had just experienced the horrors to which racial discrimination could lead? "There's no room for double standards in American politics," pronounced Senator Hubert Humphrey. "Our demands for democratic practices in other lands will be no more effective than the guarantee of those practices in our own country. . . . The time has arrived in America for the Democratic Party to get out of the shadow of states' rights and to walk forthrightly into the bright sunshine of human rights."

Small steps toward a more equitable America began to occur, though the Southern bloc stood steadfast. The federal government ended the outrageously cruel practice of leasing convicts in 1941. President Truman founded the Commission on Higher Education and the Committee on Civil Rights, which began to confront discrimination in the federal government and the armed services. These gains were nowhere near enough to level the playing field, but they breathed hopeful breath upon the glowing coals of the Civil Rights Movement.

Abroad, Communist countries began flooding the media with examples of American racism, and as the Cold War unfolded, America fumbled to counter this unflattering depiction. When *Brown v. Board of Education* ruled against school segregation, the news was loudly disseminated across the world by Voice of America. America had to demonstrate progress, concluded several State Department officials; it was a matter of national interest. Here began the propaganda narrative of racial progress and healing. Members of the Black elite were strategically held up as examples of forward momentum. The presence of successful Black entrepreneurs countered Communist accusations that the American economic system relied on racial exploitation. Wielding Black business as a political weapon would continue from this point forth. In reality, the vast majority of Black people plodded on in harsh living conditions with little hope of upward mobility.

THE ERA BETWEEN THE New Deal and the 1960s has come to be known as the "great leveling" for its historically low disparity between the wealthiest and poorest, but that shared prosperity was not shared by all. The golden age of capital was premised, in the words of Jonathan Levy, "on the white male heterosexual breadwinning wage." The massive secondary markets created by government mortgage insurance and lending programs also enriched Wall Street, making New York the world's trading capital, just as the military-industrial complex built during World War II made America the world's most powerful nation. It was all a result of massive government spending in private industry. Keynesian economics triumphed on the domestic front, and a strong domestic economy made America the world leader and the dollar the world's currency.

Yet even amid unprecedented growth and limitless money-creation power, Black Americans were left out.

CHAPTER 5

Civil Rights Dreams, Economic Nightmares

I N 1962, A YEAR BEFORE delivering his famous speech at the March on Washington, Dr. Martin Luther King Jr. delivered a lesser-known speech in New York on the centennial of the signing of the Emancipation Proclamation, in which he stated that America had failed to fulfill the mission of both the Declaration of Independence and the Emancipation Proclamation: "If we look at our history with honesty and clarity, we will be forced to admit that our federal form of government has been, from the day of its birth, weakened in its integrity, confused and confounded in its direction, by the unresolved race question." A part of the written speech that King crossed out and didn't deliver, which is still visible in his files, uses a striking metaphor: "It is as if a political thalidomide drug taken during pregnancy caused the birth of a crippled nation."

King went on to lament the income gap between Black and white workers, the large segment of unemployed Black people, and the paucity of Black bankers, Black businessmen, and a Black middle class. "If employment entails heavy work," he noted, "if wages are miserable, if the filth is revolting, the job belongs to the Negro." He called on the nation to fix the flaw in its founding documents and finally remedy its history of racism. Not just because it was morally compelling but because it was "diplomatically expedient," given the "Communist challenge" and the rise in global democracy in former colonies: "The shape of the world today does not afford us the luxury of an anemic democracy."

That same year, President John F. Kennedy vowed to "complete the work begun by Abraham Lincoln" and "eradicate the vestiges of discrimination and segregation." Kennedy not only advocated for the Civil Rights Act but envisioned broader measures to address economic inequities, declaring, a few months later, "There is little value in a Negro obtaining the right to be admitted to hotels and restaurants if he has no cash in his pocket and no job." For a moment, it seemed the nation was poised for transformation. The federal government, divided on racial issues since Reconstruction, appeared united. The Warren Court's unanimous decision in *Brown* overturned *Plessy v. Ferguson*, dismantling the legal justifications underlying the South's entire Jim Crow legal structure. The Senate, a body that acted, in the words of Robert Caro, as "the stronghold of the status quo, the dam against which the waves of social reform dashed themselves in vain," was momentarily on the side of change. Whether it was Cold War fears and the Soviets pointing out America's sordid racial history or the fact that the widespread proliferation of television had brought the long-standing struggle for equality inside every American home, the Black community's pleas for justice were finally being heard.

The Civil Rights Movement, powered by King's message of nonviolence, inspired a coalition of Black communities and white allies. The South's resistance to change appeared increasingly backward.

Landmark victories followed: the Civil Rights Act of 1964 ended seg-regation in public spaces and workplace discrimination, and the Voting Rights Act of 1965 protected Black Americans' right to vote. But though the civil rights bills eradicated the blatantly racist Jim Crow system and Northern racial covenants and "Whites Only" signs across the country, deeper economic and systemic inequalities persisted.

Financial disparities were entrenched; large gaps in wealth, income, and education persisted from a history of segregation and discrimi-nation; nearly half of Black children lived in poverty, compared to 9 percent of white children. The passage of the Civil Rights and Voting Rights Acts, though historic, did nothing to amend the fact that Black unemployment remained two times higher than white unemployment, that Black people had been almost entirely unable to accrue wealth due to the New Deal mortgage system and other barriers, that they continued to occupy low-wage jobs, or that they paid more in fees and interest rates than whites for similar goods. If, as Bayard Rustin noted, "freedom must be conceived in economic categories," then freedom for Black Americans was still a long way off.

And so it was. In the weeks following the ratification of the Civil Rights and Voting Rights Acts, unrest swept the nation. One riot in the Watts neighborhood of Los Angeles, triggered by a relatively minor instance of police aggression, resulted in numerous deaths and mil-lions of dollars' worth of property damage. Upwards of thirty thousand people participated, fueled by years of anger, resentment, and sorrow stemming from increasing poverty and segregation. And this rage was not unleashed into the void. In many cases, white business establish-ments and other properties were targeted. During a similar incident on Chicago's West Side, rioters shouted that they sought to "drive white 'exploiters' out of the ghetto." While the rioting and looting might have appeared random, studies found that the protesters were taking action against establishments that had contributed to their debt oppression. As a grocery store in Chicago went up in flames, an elderly Black man proclaimed, "Burn, burn, burn. White man ain't milking me no more."

Such rage against the Jim Crow credit market was understandable. And many white lawmakers did scramble to understand it. In 1968, the Kerner Commission led the first governmental examination of the racial wealth gap. The first draft of the report, called "The Harvest of American Racism," contained such a scathing denouncement of the Great Society programs for their sheer ineffectuality in tackling the problem—that is, in leaving white racist institutions intact—that all 120 social scientists involved were fired. The Kerner report offered three future scenarios: maintaining the status quo, which would result in more violence; enrichment of the ghettos, which would lead to a "permanently divided country"; or complete integration. The commission resolutely endorsed this final option, which would bring about "a single society, in which every citizen will be free to live and work according to his capabilities and desires, not his color."

The Senate also commissioned studies that focused on the disparate economics of the ghetto, which had been created thanks to the white affirmative action programs of the New Deal. Black households carried disproportionately higher levels of installment debt compared to white households, which significantly curtailed their disposable income, as a greater share of earnings was diverted toward servicing interest on accumulating debt. A series of studies by Columbia sociologist David Caplovitz, published in 1967 as *The Poor Pay More*, and by the Federal Trade Commission (FTC), found that white suburbanites were buying consumer goods much more cheaply than one could in the ghetto, generally for products of better quality, and that the poor, specifically those residing in the ghetto, were paying more for goods across the board. This had everything to do with the bifurcated system of credit established through New Deal programs, as well as the compounding effects of the racial wealth gap. Upwards of 90 percent of consumer goods and necessities purchased in the ghetto were acquired through installment credit, compared to around 20 percent in the white suburbs. The studies also found that the ghetto-bound poor—a captive market—paid much more for lower-quality necessities like food, medicine, and dental care.

An "urban sharecropping system" had begun to develop, wherein ghetto residents were preyed on by exploitative lenders promising to ease the burden of their debt. To make matters worse, because retailers in the ghetto often sold low-quality merchandise, ghetto consumers found themselves with broken or faulty purchases before they had even finished paying for them. They would then default, increasing the restrictions on their future credit. Repossession, wage garnishment—which often led to job loss—and even shakedowns were common, as were court judgments to address loan default, dragging law enforcement into the Black credit quagmire.

Given these circumstances, lenders in the ghetto were an obvious target for urban rioters. But no one—not even these predatory lenders, who were undeniably taking advantage of the poor—was profiting from this broken system. Wealth was simply too scarce. As the debt historian Louis Hyman noted, "Between bad debt losses, lawyers' collection fees, higher insurance premiums, more accounting staff, and higher sales commissions, the higher costs of ghetto retailers accounted for 94 percent of the difference in the gross margins." While the rest of the country got increasingly comfortable in the modern credit cycle, luxuriously outfitted in secondary markets and undergirded by large

and powerful finance companies that lowered risks and costs, both customers and lenders in the ghetto continued to flail.

THE REASONS FOR THIS glaring disparity were known at the time.
As the Kerner Commission experts had concluded, income and opportunity inequality had created the rift, which was ever-widening. Even
a patching of the income gap would be insufficient; the only possible
solution was developing government-backed initiatives to reverse past
privileges.

Two hearings were held in the wake of the riots to grapple with
ghetto inequity. Both were led by Wisconsin Senator William Proxmire, an incorruptible Democrat committed to fixing the injustices of
the credit system. He and his team had come to understand that the
"economic illness of the ghetto" was steadily worsening due to the toxic
credit cycle. It became clear during the hearings that Black exploitation at the hands of white institutions was the source of the economic
malady and resulting unrest. "Soul brother establishments," as the few
Black-owned businesses that survived in the ghetto were called, were
largely spared destruction and looting. The solution seemed clear: more
Black businesses and financial institutions in the inner city. Unfortunately, the illness had been misdiagnosed. While there was indeed a
dearth of healthy Black-owned businesses, ghetto interest rates were
responsible for the diseased ghetto economy, not the race of the lenders.

Jacob Javits, a Republican senator from New York, proposed a
plan that would provide federal backing to Black-owned businesses.
He believed that "no conceivable increase in the gross national product
would stir these backwaters" without such an intervention. The Small
Business Administration (SBA) responded by creating a lending and
financial education program called Project OWN, designed to bring

about "economic emancipation" for Black Americans. Proxmire, who believed strongly in credit unions, put forth a bill "designed to help the poor break out of this vicious cycle" by "authorizing a strong federal program to encourage the formation of credit unions and consumer counseling programs for the poor." But this program relied on a pooling of community resources—which were, as had always been the case, insufficient to the task. The notion that local control of collective capital would eventually allow impoverished communities to participate in the economy was a myth. Credit unions had indeed helped the middle class, but this help had originated in federally subsidized mortgages, not the collection of meager finances.

Though misguided about the efficacy of credit unions for ameliorating ghetto economics, Proxmire would go on to contribute significantly to the elimination of credit discrimination through various fair lending bills, which ended race and gender discrimination in lending. By the 1970s, lenders could no longer deny credit because of race or gender. However, anti-discrimination provisions were not enough to fix the intricately entangled economic horror in which poor Black Americans were caught. Just as removing the legal enforcements of Jim Crow segregation had not drained racism from the groundwater, legislation aimed at credit discrimination couldn't dissolve the complex financial problems of the ghetto.

In yet another misinformed and ineffectual attempt to fix the situation, the FTC pushed for financial education projects. Similar to Project OWN's lending and counseling programs, this effort was based on the notion that Black people were simply making bad financial decisions. The FTC's subsequent study, however, revealed that this was not the case. The survey found that 85 percent of ghetto consumers thought it was a "good idea" to buy on credit only in very particular circumstances, and an outright bad idea otherwise. They bought on credit and sank further into debt for one reason and one reason only: there was no other option.

Two potential solutions to reduce the credit disparity, were in fact available, but neither one ever made it into law, because of political unviability. The first, to integrate the credit market, would have required physical integration. The second, to lay a foundation for wealth growth by actually providing capital to the poor Black community, went against the grain of color-blind equality. Though the Lyndon B. Johnson administration launched various robust "War on Poverty'" programs within his Great Society programs, Congress maintained that "these are not programs to bring about major structural change in the economy or to generate large numbers of additional jobs." In general, Johnson's Great Society lacked wealth-building initiatives, which would have been instrumental in reducing the racial wealth gap.

Johnson did seem to genuinely see and lament the economic injustice Black Americans faced. He even seemed to understand that there was a fundamental difference between Black and white poverty. In a speech at Howard University, he admitted that the crippling poverty in which so many Black people were drowning was a result of the "devastating heritage of long years of slavery; and a century of oppression, hatred, and injustice." He attested that "you do not take a person who, for years, has been hobbled by chains and liberate him, bring him up to the starting line of a race and then say, 'you are free to compete with all the others,' and still justly believe that you have been completely fair." Here, he was directly quoting King, who said, "If a man is entering the starting line in a race three hundred years after another man, the first would have to perform some impossible feat in order to catch up with his fellow runner."

Yet, within the same speech, Johnson simultaneously offered an opposing view on the cause of Black poverty: that it stemmed from the deterioration of Black family, cultural malaise, and other moral failings in the Black community. And here, he was quoting the other theory for the racial wealth gap, one offered by white policymakers at the time, which blamed not a history of exclusion but, unsurprisingly, Black people themselves for having less money than whites.

In 1965, Daniel Patrick Moynihan, the assistant secretary of labor, drafted a report titled *The Negro Family: The Case for National Action*, in which he proclaimed that urban violence was a result of the "tangle of pathology" inherent in Black culture. This destructive theory continues to permeate the ways in which poverty is analyzed today. Moynihan pointed directly at high rates of single motherhood and other indicators of Black family breakdown, calling it "the principal source of most of the aberrant, inadequate, or anti-social behavior that . . . serves to perpetuate the cycle of poverty and deprivation." The report, which for generations would deeply inform policy and the lens through which Americans viewed Black poverty—was cited as primary evidence in a 2014 congressional budget report. The time for government reckoning with the atrocities of slavery and the subsequent economic suffocation of the Black community had passed.

THE SENTIMENTS BEHIND THE Watts Riot and other such outbursts of destruction was certainly not unfounded, but their manifestation played a significant part in fracturing the civil rights coalition. King attempted to quell the rapidly mounting storm, as did other leaders of the movement, professing to hear the protesters' righteous outcry while urging them to seek peaceful solutions. But this new wave of resistance surged around them, unabated. King tried, too, to turn the

public eye toward the persistent "daily violence" endured by Black people in the form of destitution, segregation, and unemployment, but this
tactic did not hold, either.

The tide was turning yet again. A poll taken in 1966 found that 85
percent of whites felt "the pace of civil rights progress was too fast." The
solidarity that had felt so strong only a few years before was dwindling,
displaced by a baseless fear that white gains would diminish if Black
gains increased. Most of these fears were manufactured by politicians
who benefited from the political weapon of white supremacy. Barry
Goldwater jump-started the libertarian agenda during his failed presidential run in the mid-1960s; the movement would continue to swell.
By infusing his libertarian rhetoric with opposition to civil rights,
integration, and government efforts to counteract poverty, Goldwater
roped the South back into the Republican Party.

Though devout allegiance to free-market capitalism might well
have stemmed from the "threat" of communism, it quickly came to
entail a rejection of the Black Power movement's requests for Black economic justice. Reagan would take this specific mix and run with it. He,
George Wallace, Pat Buchanan, and Richard Nixon all specialized in
appeals to a "silent (white) majority" against radical Black troublemak-
ers, a winning Republican political strategy that Nixon would perfect
to recapture the South for a generation. The utility of white supremacy
had not diminished in the least, especially when it helped the white
elite maintain a political structure that benefited a wealthy minority.
Not only did ramping up racial hatred allow white policymakers to do
nothing in terms of racial redress for Black America; it also allowed
them to roll back the Keynesian mixed economy that had built the
middle class and taxed the über-wealthy out of existence. Once again,
the white poor received the wages of whiteness for handing over their

unions, pensions, and job security. The convenient argument that race-focused policy perpetuates racial othering and, thus, discrimination was born of this fear and lingers with surprising vigor today.

THE BACKLASH TO CIVIL rights began so quickly after the passage of the Civil Rights and Voting Rights Acts that it allowed those in power to claim a Pyrrhic victory while ignoring the central issue of the racial divide. Though some progress was certainly made, the first iteration of the movement had established a focus on legal and political equality, not economic equality. And perhaps most tragically, the urban uprisings had brought about a fresh horror for Black people: a police state.

It was during this era that welfare came to be associated with Black poverty and fell out of favor. Even though it failed to provide targeted assistance to Black communities, conservatives lambasted the War on Poverty for its "handouts." The War on Poverty swiftly folded into the burgeoning War on Crime—politicians wishing to stoke racial resentment highlighted instances of lawlessness and crime that accompanied the nationwide protests rather than the conditions that had led to the protests. Funds that had been set aside for poverty-reduction programs were used, instead, to bolster law enforcement. Black community surveillance increased and, with it, the criminalization of Black life and the long-lasting misassociation between Blackness and criminality. Even worse, a new justification for racial hierarchy was born. White supremacists craftily slipped into the front lines of the War on Crime, changing their rhetoric to match the new rationale for Black oppression. Ronald Reagan's campaign for governor was emblazoned with riot footage and a deeply disturbing tagline: "Every day the jungle draws a little closer."

ONE OF THE MOST powerful agents at work in the oppression of Black Americans—then and now—was the rewriting of history. Martin Luther King's decades of tireless, groundbreaking work and leadership were gradually stripped down to one sentence of his famous "I Have a Dream Speech": "I have a dream that my four little children will one day live in a nation where they will not be judged by the color of their skin but by the content of their character." Before long, not a trace of his vehement condemnation of America's long legacy of injustice remained. A drastically watered-down and conveniently nebulous plea for a color-blind utopia, extrapolated from one admittedly beautiful sentence, took the place of his specific demands for economic change.

King, who drew influence from Mahatma Gandhi's nonviolent revolution against British colonialism, understood that "the underlying purpose of segregation was to oppress and exploit the segregated, not simply to keep them apart. . . . The basic purpose of segregation was to perpetuate injustice and inequality." Frustrated at the loss of momentum—both social and political—in the wake of the Civil Rights Act, King gave another speech, on Independence Day 1965:

> About two years ago now . . . I tried to tell the nation about a dream I had. I must confess to you this morning that since that sweltering August afternoon in 1963, my dream has often turned into a nightmare; I've seen it shattered. . . . I continue to see it shattered as I walk through the Harlems of our nation and see sometimes ten and fifteen Negroes trying to live in one or two rooms. I've been down to the Delta of Mississippi since then, and I've seen my dream shattered as I met hundreds of people who didn't earn more than six or seven dollars a week. I've seen my dream shattered as I've walked the

streets of Chicago and seen Negroes, young men and women, with a sense of utter hopelessness because they can't find any jobs. And they see life as a long and desolate corridor with no exit signs.

King's desolation should surprise no one. Life in the ghetto had continued its downward spiral while white America was riding high on the postwar economic boom. To a person who had fought so hard to better his country for his people, who had ushered in an era that appeared to be a real turning point, the continued harsh reality for Black Americans—especially when held in contrast against the prosperity enjoyed by most white Americans—must have made him feel that his life's work had been all but futile.

Shortly before he was killed, King began organizing a "Poor People's Campaign," which aimed to address poverty experienced by all races. Gerald McKnight writes that "King was proposing nothing less than a radical transformation of the Civil Rights Movement into a populist crusade calling for redistribution of economic and political power." In his final speech before his murder, King urged a bank boycott in support of the Memphis sanitation workers' strike; called a "bank-in," the boycott would have the local Black community withdraw their deposits from white-owned institutions and place them in Memphis's only Black-owned bank. He closed the speech with a note of premonition and hope:

Like anybody, I would like to live a long life. Longevity has its place. But I'm not concerned about that now. I just want to do God's will. And He's allowed me to go up to the mountain. And I've looked over. And I've seen the promised land. I may not get there with you. But I want you to know tonight, that we, as a people, will get to the promised land.

And I'm happy, tonight. I'm not worried about anything. I'm not fearing any man. Mine eyes have seen the glory of the coming of the Lord.

King was assassinated the next day: April 4, 1968. Without him, the Civil Rights Movement he had been so instrumental in creating began to crumble. A more confrontational movement, infused with Malcolm X's vision of Black revolution, swelled in its wake. Stokely Carmichael made clear their demands: "We want Black Power." He and the other new Black leaders saw that "the economic foundations of this country must be shaken if black people are to control their lives." In his haunting work *The Fire Next Time*, James Baldwin explored this shift: "Crime became real, for example—for the first time—not as a possibility but as the possibility. One would never defeat one's circumstances by working and saving one's pennies; one would never, by working, acquire that many pennies, and, besides, the social treatment accorded even the most successful Negroes proved that one needed, in order to be free, something more than a bank account. One needed a handle, a lever, a means of inspiring fear."

Malcolm X was intimately familiar with the ghetto and all its traps. To him, equal rights were beside the point, because "the [U.S.] government [had] proven itself either unwilling or unable to defend the lives and the property of Negroes." He saw full-scale revolution as the only path forward. Like King, he also called for Black economic liberation through Black-owned business. "Our people have to be made to see," he said, "that any time you take your dollar out of your community and spend it in a community where you don't live, the community where you live will get poorer and poorer, and the community where you spend your money will get richer and richer." Unlike King, though,

Malcolm was not convinced that the radical changes that were necessary could be achieved through nonviolence.

Huey Newton approached the desperate need for change by co-founding the Black Panther Party with the aim of organizing and mobilizing the ghetto. The Panthers, like Malcolm X, wanted a revolution. They produced a list of Black needs and wants, largely encompassed by the final point: "We want land, bread, housing, education, clothing, justice and peace." They also made clear their complete severance of allegiance to the American government, proclaiming, "Whenever any form of government becomes destructive of these ends, it is the right of people to alter or to abolish it, and to institute new government, laying its foundations on such principles and organizing its powers in such form as to them shall seem more likely to affect their safety and happiness." The Panthers' declaration mirrored exactly the claims of Thomas Jefferson two hundred years prior. That declaration, written by a man not unaware of the hypocrisies of extolling equality and freedom while holding men in chains, was being summoned again as a reminder of the nation's core tenets. Like King, the Panthers simply used the promises of America's founding documents to hold the country to task.

To achieve constitutional equality, however, required justice. Justice to remedy the years of exploitation, discrimination, and segregation that had created such stark racial inequalities. Once justice was achieved between the races, race would no longer be useful as a potent political weapon. The myths of racial hierarchy would fall, just as King had envisioned in his dream. There would be no need to justify such stark economic inequalities if those inequalities were remedied. That was justice: to make things fair, to break the association of Black and poor and white and rich, so that every child could achieve according to their own merit rather than the color of their skin. The main obstacle to achieving justice was not economic; America had time and again proved capable of creating wealth through programs that benefited many—the New Deal, the Homestead Acts, the wartime mixed economy, and on and on. Yet, as during Reconstruction, justice was denied through the fruitful politics of white supremacy. Racism was stoked in order to maintain the status quo.

It is important, however, to understand that the economics of justice were not difficult. Justice for Black Americans would not have, as race-baiting politicians insinuated, come at the expense of white Americans. American leaders faced a choice in the 1960s: expand the pie, as the New Deal had done, to reach all Americans, which would require a shift in spending from the war to domestic issues and the integration of employment, credit markets, and neighborhood, or do nothing.

By the mid- to late 1960s, the U.S. economy was still expanding, and there was no inherent reason federal policy could not continue to stimulate growth while also addressing the racial exclusions of the past. The New Deal and wartime economies had already proven that state-led investment—guided by Keynesian principles—was a powerful engine of prosperity. What the civil rights laws of the 1960s made newly possible was a redirection of those public funds toward the Black communities that had long been excluded. Before neoliberalism took hold—prioritizing market discipline over social equity—lawmakers were already experimenting with ways to extend the public credit franchise to marginalized groups.

The path forward was not mysterious; the New Deal had offered a template for using government credit and investment to expand opportunity. Policymakers had numerous tools at their disposal to foster shared growth. One idea was to direct federal resources to the inner cities, just as earlier programs had built the white suburbs. In 1968, Republican Senator Jacob Javits and Texas Senator John Tower partnered with CORE's Roy Innis to propose the Community Self-Determination Bill, which Javits described as a Marshall Plan for Black America. Other proposals included extending job guarantees to the Black poor through King's Poor People's Campaign, launching a development finance institution modeled on the Export-Import Bank to fund urban infrastructure, and advancing housing integration—an agenda promoted by Johnson's Fair Housing Act and embraced by Republican presidential candidates like George Romney.

IT ALSO SEEMED LOGICAL that the white credit system the lawmakers had created should be tweaked slightly to include the Americans left out of it. There were more than twenty civil rights reforms between 1968 and 1988 that declared and implemented citizens' "right" to bank without discrimination. The largest and most important were the Fair Housing Act of 1968, the Equal Credit Opportunity Act of 1974, the Home Mortgage Disclosure Act of 1975, and the Community Reinvestment Act of 1977. Aside from civil rights reforms, there were many other credit needs across the economy. As Greta Krippner recounts in *Capitalizing on Crisis*, "Credit allocation schemes were continually on the legislative agenda from the mid-1960s to the mid-1970s, with nearly 100 separate bills under consideration in the 1974 legislative session alone." Although they varied in detail, notes Krippner, "the basic premise was the same: if government controls in the form of Regulation Q ceilings were distorting flows of credit in the economy, then government actions could be devised to counteract the distortion, directing scarce capital where it was needed." Or as Senator Proxmire put it: there is a "widely shared assumption" that "a [bank's] public charter conveys numerous economic benefits and in return it is legitimate for public policy and regulatory practice to require some public purpose." The senator asserted here an already fading view of banks as "a franchise to serve local convenience and needs"; therefore, "it is fair for the public to ask something in return."

It was more than fair. The state, having created the economy, had a right to re-edit it. It could prohibit bank discrimination, as Proxmire and Congress had done, but it could also change monetary policy—it could create more credit: stop crucifying mankind on a cross of gold. Or change the basis of the economy from war and the cross of iron to the War on Poverty. After the 1965 Watts Riot, Congressman August Hawkins, a Black civil rights leader from the Watts neighborhood, joined forces with Democratic presidential nominee and former vice president Hubert Humphrey to propose several remedies to low unemployment, including using monetary policy to loosen money to create jobs. Their campaign came to be labeled "a Black issue" among lawmakers and was significantly watered down. The final bill, which passed in 1978, directed the Federal Reserve to focus on a dual mandate of securing full employment and controlling inflation. However, in the time it took to debate and pass the bill through Congress, the neoliberal transformation of monetary policy was completed.

As some Black activists intuited, the federal government could simply turn the great engine of the mixed economy, which had created so much wealth during the world war, on America's inner cities. However, to do so would have required a turning away from the racial divisions and myths that had sustained American politics since Reconstruction. It also would have meant turning away from the lucrative and politically powerful military-industrial complex. "That was the problem—money," said Lyndon B. Johnson about the Kerner Commission's proposals, even as he spent hundreds of billions on war.

It was a matter not of money per se—the government does not have a limited budget—but, rather, of general societal and political resources. Should the government spend its resources and the people's on guns or schools? In his 1953 speech "The Chance for Peace," President Dwight Eisenhower had laid out the central tension in government spending: "The cost of one modern heavy bomber is this: a modern brick school in more than 30 cities. It is two electric power plants, each serving a town of 60,000 population. It is two fine, fully equipped hospitals. It is some 50 miles of concrete highway. We pay for a single fighter plane with a half million bushels of wheat. We pay for a single destroyer with new homes that could have housed more than 8,000 people." The nation's wealth and technological advancement had given the country the capacity, as King remarked in his 1962 Emancipation Proclamation speech, "to rebuild our whole planet, filling it with luxury—or the capacity to destroy it totally."

It was more than just a resource problem. As Eisenhower recognized, the "military-industrial complex," the private corporations and government apparatus built to finance a war, had grown too large and powerful. It would fight for its own survival and profitability even when war had become unnecessary. Eisenhower, a military commander, urged the nation to change its focus, warning ominously, "Under the cloud of threatening war, it is humanity hanging from a cross of iron." The imagery was reminiscent of William Jennings Bryan's "cross of gold"—both alluding to an unjustified collective sacrifice. With the gold standard, the nation's farmers were deprived to feed gold reserves; likewise, the military-industrial complex made profits for private industry at the cost of human lives and other societal imperatives, like schools and hospitals. "I knew that America would never invest the necessary funds or energies in rehabilitation of its poor so long as adventures like Vietnam continued to draw men and skills and money like some demonic, destructive suction tube," said King.

America's postwar history proved that public spending could spur a virtuous economic cycle and increase the size of the pie. Black communities were seeking the same kinds of jobs and mortgages that had created the white middle class. However, not only was this path not taken, but the very real possibility that the federal government would channel resources to Black communities resulted in a political backlash that eroded the political majorities that had voted for and benefited from the New Deal's mixed economy.

CHAPTER 6

The Decoy of Black Capitalism

E QUIPPED WITH SHARP POLITICAL INSTINCTS and unfettered by scruples, President Nixon navigated the murky climate he inherited from Johnson by simultaneously opposing legal race discrimination and shutting down government integration initiatives. Nixon understood that his only path to an electoral majority was through white backlash—he needed to take the George Wallace Dixiecrats and secure the Southern states. Wallace, the Democratic governor of Alabama, who had famously stood in front of a schoolhouse door and shouted, "Segregation now, segregation tomorrow, segregation forever"—was a front-runner for the 1968 Republican presidential primary. His campaign was built on white Americans' fears of change, a fear that had hardened—thanks in part to his own efforts—into rage and resentment.

In the South, it only helped Wallace to be explicit in his racism. But in the North, race-baiting wouldn't land in the same manner. Alan Greenspan, a Nixon campaign adviser, counseled Nixon to "be loud enough for the George Wallace leaners to hear us, yet protect ourselves from charges of distortion"; to denounce Wallace's "amateurism" and to avoid talk of matching violence with violence (which would scare "the housewife"); but to go after the voters who sought "the emotional satisfaction" of seeing sheriffs "knocking heads" after every riot.

THE WAY TO OVERCOME the chaos of rebellion was to harness its energy. If Black Americans were angry about being exploited for so long, well, so too were the whites of the "silent majority," which was being overlooked and neglected because other groups were making so much noise. The Nixon campaign's research director and media analyst, Pat Buchanan, followed up in writing that it was "vital" that Nixon listen to Greenspan's polling data and forget about ever getting "the Negro vote," which he said was lost to the Republicans "for a generation." If Black issues mattered at all, it was only because "the Negro loud-mouths are given access to the public communications media by a guilt-ridden establishment."

As Dwight Eisenhower's vice president, Nixon had worked with Congress to pass civil rights legislation, met with Martin Luther King, and even gained Jackie Robinson's endorsement during his 1960 campaign against Kennedy. By the time he became the Republican presidential candidate in 1968, however, his message about racial justice would be much clearer. As Robinson summarized it in a 1968 article revoking his support, "The Republican Party has told the black man to go to hell. I offer to them a similar invitation." Nixon chose race-baiting as a political strategy. And it was a successful one.

Days after the July 1967 riot in Newark, New Jersey, Buchanan called Greenspan to request his advice on devising economic-assistance programs that would deal with the race issue while also sounding fiscally responsible—that is, Buchanan (and Nixon) sought a politically

palatable program of economic aid. However, the free-market funda-
mentalist responded with a provocation: "The negro problem is not an
economic problem and it is dangerous to think of its solution in financial terms." Greenspan argued that *government aid*, rather than a solution to the problem of racial unrest, was the problem. He felt welfare
and entitlements created dependence, and told the Nixon team that
Black families were relatively well-off compared to, for example, Black
populations in other regions of the world. What created the anger
that led to violence was not poverty but *anti-poverty* programs, which
stoked racism and "class antagonism." At the time, this was a view far
from the mainstream and far from what even Nixon or Buchanan had
in mind. But it worked like a charm. Thus was born "Black capitalism,"
Nixon's signature program to deal with the race issue: it would amount
to nothing in terms of progress, but it would yield long-lasting results
in terms of stoking "the culture wars" by giving the appearance that
Black Americans were getting special treatment.

Nixon's Black capitalism was rooted firmly in neoliberal ideology,
the idea that the best policy to any societal dilemma was to unleash the
free market to reach maximum efficiency. Yet Nixon's commitment to
neoliberalism was haphazard and surface level. It was not *free-market
capitalism* he wanted but *Black capitalism*. He increased the size of the
federal government, installed price controls, ended the gold standard,
and violated almost every tenet held dear by neoliberals, even declaring
himself to be a Keynesian. Nixon was not a true believer in the free
market or, likely, anything else; rather, he was a connoisseur of détente
and decoy, and he spotted in free-market economics a politically savvy,
data-backed passage through a political thicket.

The Nixon administration's carefully finessed Black capitalist
agenda was amorphous enough to be interpreted in various ways. Nix-

on's rhetoric seemed to promote Black advancement, while appealing to those alarmed by urban violence and those who valued American allegiance to upward mobility. "Instead of government jobs, and government housing, and government welfare," proclaimed Nixon, upon his acceptance of the Republican nomination, "let government use its tax and credit policies to enlist in this battle the greatest engine of progress ever developed in the history of man—American private enterprise." In these words, Americans of all stripes heard what they wanted to hear.

Black leaders had certainly been calling for the enrichment of Black business, but what they wanted was, as activist Roy Innis put it, the "transfer of institutions within the black community to the management and control of the people themselves." Nixon was not interested in that level of involvement. His Black capitalism project would receive little federal aid and would put the onus of amending the "Black problem" almost entirely on the shoulders of the Black community.

In keeping with the logic of Daniel Patrick Moynihan, Nixon's Council of Urban Affairs head, who believed that "the time may have come when the issue of race could benefit from a period of 'benign neglect,'" Nixon would keep the promise he made Southern Republicans to "lay off pro-Negro crap" and neglect what he saw as politically ineffectual cooperation with Black leaders. And not only would he halt government involvement in racial justice; he would actively roll progress back. Under his leadership, Black activism lost the national stage, the Voting Rights Act was severely curtailed, and Johnson's Great Society programs went largely unfunded.

For a moment during the Johnson presidency, it had seemed as if government-assisted integration might have been on the horizon. Despite vigorous pushback from Congress and lobby groups, Johnson worked actively against housing segregation. A week after Martin

Luther King was killed, he passed the Fair Housing Act. This law, which Johnson considered the most crucial piece of civil rights legislation his administration managed to enact, prohibited racial discrimination in housing. But Nixon's position on integration was crystal clear: he would not wield his presidential power to implement it.

Unfortunately for Nixon, his Housing and Urban Development director, George Romney, saw that integration would not occur without government intervention. Unlike the president, who'd won the GOP nomination in 1968 through exploitative opportunism, Romney lost it while standing fast to his moderate Republican ideals. He openly disavowed the Southern strategy and tried to open Republicans to the civil rights cause. With zealous conviction and without seeking permission from the White House, he pursued the Fair Housing Act's promise "affirmatively to further" fair housing. As HUD director, he mandated the rejection of project applications submitted by states or municipalities that maintained segregated housing practices—until Nixon found out and put an end to it.

The next item on Romney's agenda was even more pointed: a community "in which choices are available, doors are unlocked, opportunities exist for those who have felt walled within the ghetto." Called the "Open Communities" plan, its purpose was to finally move Black residents out of the ghettos and into the suburbs. The plan would be tackled with the construction of public housing in the suburbs and the extension of loans to Black people.

Romney launched the project in several communities across the country, including Warren, Michigan, which was rife with mounting racial tension. When he announced that he would be withholding $3 million in federal funds unless the city embraced subsidized housing, the population erupted in enraged resistance. Undeterred, Romney pushed on, even going so far as to bring a bill to Congress without the president's blessing. The bill, an ambitious attempt to bolster the Fair Housing Act, was shut down by the Senate Banking Committee.

Nixon maintained that he was "convinced that while legal segregation is totally wrong [but] that forced integration of housing or education is just as wrong," even though he "realize[d] that this position will lead us to a situation in which blacks will continue to live for the most part in black neighborhoods and where there will be predominantly black schools and predominately white schools." What's more, Nixon's cunning political mind understood what Romney's moral vantage point allowed him to ignore: pushing integration was political suicide. After numerous attempts to get Romney off his back, Nixon resolved the "Romney problem" by appointing him ambassador to Mexico, effectively ending Romney's career and extinguishing what remained of moderate conservatism.

With Romney gone, Nixon continued to uphold the FHA only in cases of flagrant discrimination, which meant that communities could bar low-income housing and keep their whiteness intact. When the Supreme Court upheld *James v. Valtierra*, which permitted a town in California to prohibit public housing, the law of the land was made clear: minorities could be effectively kept out as long as the law was not explicitly racist. In the words of Dempsey Travis: "John Fitzgerald Kennedy turned on the light at the end of the housing corridor for black Americans. Lyndon Johnson kept it burning but Richard Milhous Nixon turned it off in the 1970s."

As Roy Innis put it, "Integration is dead as a doornail." Black leaders stopped asking to be included in white America and again fixed their sights on economic self-determination. Stokely Carmichael articulated this position succinctly: "We should begin with the basic fact that black Americans have two problems: they are poor and they are black. But integration speaks not at all to the problem of poverty, only to the problem of blackness. Integration today means the man who 'makes it,' leaving his black brothers behind in the ghetto as fast as his new sports car will take him." Though astute in many ways, this sentiment overlooked the ways in which poverty and segregation had indeed become comorbidities for Black people. Each issue was detrimental and unique in its own right, but historically and culturally entangled with its counterpart.

What had become undeniable, though, was the ever-widening economic disparity between Black and white Americans—as well as the dramatic correlation between money and political power. Additionally, the rise in urban violence had demonstrated that legal rights were simply not enough to appease a community that continued to endure insurmountable economic hardship. At the National Black Economic Development Conference, which was held on the first anniversary of King's death, the shift from a focus on legal equality to economic advancement was palpable. During the conference, James Forman delivered his "Black Manifesto" housed within a speech entitled "Total Control as the Only Solution for the Economic Needs of Black People." It was an outright call for reparations; Foreman demanded "$15 per nigger" from religious institutions that participated in the capitalist exploitation of Black labor.

OTHER EFFORTS TOWARD SECURING reparations were afoot, too. The Republic of New Africa was an organization forged by Black separatists to create a sovereign nation in the South with money gleaned from the American government. The economist Richard F. America Jr.

suggested that the government turn a number of Fortune 500 companies over to Black control. Dunbar S. McLaurin offered the "Ghetto Economic Development and Industrialization Plan" to help develop the ghetto using outside funds.

While talking out of the side of his mouth about Black capitalism, Nixon persisted in his underlying two-pronged approach to race. His first tactic, to forge an association between Blackness and crime, allowed him to boast of a unique ability to establish and maintain "law and order," thus securing him the support of scared white voters. The other, to link Blackness to welfare dependence, circularly bolstered his case for Black capitalism. He slipped this rhetoric into speeches and campaign ads. One such ad featured images of predominantly Black and brown poor people, undergirded by his voice. "For the past five years we've been deluged by programs for the unemployed—programs for the cities—programs for the poor," he explained. "And we have reaped from these programs an ugly harvest of frustration, violence, and failure across the land."

In one fell swoop, Nixon conflated the uptick in violence with government assistance rather than its actual cause: abject poverty. He insisted that the government's "overpromising and under-producing" had brought about the violence, announced that "Civil Rights is no longer an issue," then swiftly turned the spotlight on the Black community itself. Black people, attested Nixon, "do not want more government programs which perpetuate dependency. They don't want to be a colony in a nation. They want the pride, and the self-respect, and the dignity that can only come if they have an equal chance to own their own homes, to own their own businesses, to be managers and executives as well as workers, to have a piece of the action in the exciting ventures of private enterprise." Just like Andrew Johnson vetoing the land grant while admonishing freed men to rely on capitalism, Nixon cut the Civil Rights Movement short before it got to economic redress while gaslighting the Black community about personal responsibility and the "dignity" of self-help.

Nixon's commitments to the free market were shallow—he called himself a Keynesian, ended the gold standard, and imposed price controls, but when it came to helping Black communities, he sided with the libertarians in his administration, who admonished him to do nothing. As had always been the case, Black Americans were being urged to participate in a capitalist system that continued to bar them from equal—if any—participation. This time, though, they were expected to succeed on their own, and they were shamed for holding themselves back by not having done so yet. And yet, Black capitalism helped Nixon win the White House. Even the *New York Times* claimed that Nixon's radio speech "on the need for the development of black capitalism and ownership in the ghetto may prove to be more constructive than anything yet said by other Presidential candidates on the crisis of the cities."

Nixon's Black capitalism propaganda gained instant traction with Republicans, who understood how politically savvy it was—and how cheap. The nebulous nature of the "program" was meant to inspire hope in the concept of Black businesses, not fund them. Indeed, the sticker price was as minuscule as the gains. Nixon gave the Office of Minority Business Enterprise (OMBE), which he initiated in 1969, the directive to seek financial backing from private businesses and other federal agencies. He did not give the OMBE any direct funding. Indeed, shortly after its founding, Nixon lost all interest in the OMBE.

Some members of the Nixon administration, however, became genuinely interested in and committed to the Black capitalism initiative. Theodore Cross, Nixon's key adviser on Black capitalism, saw the ghetto trap for what it was and thought the government should put significant capital toward fortifying the ghetto economy. He also saw that the trap was perpetuated by white gatekeepers, and that there was a dearth of demand for Black businesses. To elucidate this last observation, he used sports as an analogy. Until the 1960s, Cross pointed out, discrimination had greatly curtailed the market for Black athletes. However, as soon as demand grew, so did the number of Black athletes.

Of course, demand for Black businesses had long been scarce. As Cross wrote, the paucity of Black businesses was an "assured economic result of the sustained and collective preference of white people not to trade or exchange commercial promises with black people."

The OMBE put forth several valiant attempts to actually do the work the committee had been designed to do, but all of them failed or were swiftly shut down by Maurice Stans, the Republican bureaucrat Nixon had placed in charge. Stans reiterated that the program was designed to "create pride among the minority which, in turn, creates aspirations of those down the line," not to provide financial support. In other words, Black capitalism was to remain a PR stunt.

The recession of the early 1970s affected most of the country, but, predictably, it hit Black businesses the hardest. Any OMBE programs that had seen even minor success before the recession were focused on small business support, yet small businesses stood no chance in a recession economy when even large businesses were failing. The ethos that local, small businesses were the beating heart of America's entrepreneur-oriented capitalism remained an integral part of the country's narrative, but this rhetoric did not ameliorate the economic pressures that were making small businesses increasingly obsolete. This was the era in which multinational enterprises like Wal-Mart were gaining traction in America.

Moynihan oversaw the genesis of a program (referred to as the "set-aside program") designed to provide contracts to minority small businesses, and it allocated more funds to minority businesses than to any other. And yet the $66 million it handed out in contracts to these businesses in 1971 was only *one-tenth of 1 percent* of the total amount of federal contracts distributed that year. To make matters worse, studies found that 20 percent of this slim margin of contracts had in fact gone to white-owned businesses, and that Nixon had exchanged some of these contracts for political leverage. Still, the program was met with conservative ire and accusations of "preferential treatment" for minorities.

Affirmative action was yet another puzzle piece in the Black capitalism tableau. Title VII of the Civil Rights Act established the Equal Employment Opportunity Commission (EEOC), which had a mandate to take "affirmative action" to combat employment discrimination. Widespread racial bias in hiring practices and union membership had, after all, sparked the 1963 March on Washington for Jobs and Freedom, which had led to the passage of the civil rights laws. Under President Johnson, measures to address workplace discrimination included imposing fines or sanctions on employers and enacting affirmative action mandates for housing integration.

George Romney was the only member of Nixon's cabinet who took these housing mandates seriously. In contrast, Nixon's labor secretary, George Shultz, approached these challenges with strategic pragmatism. A Chicago economist and a close ally of Milton Friedman and George Stigler's, Shultz spearheaded the Office of Management and Budget (OMB), which would become central to the rise of neoliberalism. Shultz also proposed the 1969 Philadelphia Plan, which introduced hiring quotas for federal contractors and encouraged minority business procurement programs—or "set asides"—to support minority entrepreneurs. However, as soon as the word "quotas" surfaced, unions and congressional Republicans raised an outcry about what they called "special treatment." In response, the administration replaced direct mandates with softer language, urging corporations and federal agencies to "volunteer" efforts to "promote," "assist," "advise," and "encourage" minority hiring without providing funding or substantive investment. As one Columbia law professor noted, under these strategies, an employer with "about the 'right' proportion" of minorities would become "virtually invulnerable to a charge of discrimination."

Several companies, including AT&T, General Electric, and Coors, began publicizing their "minority hiring" programs through advertisements. While these campaigns often stemmed from legal settlements with the Department of Justice, they gave the impression of significant progress. In reality, as National Urban League President Whitney Young pointed out in a 1970 *New York Times* op-ed, these initiatives amounted to little more than "two dozen summer jobs" in select cities.

What the public saw, however, was widespread corporate admiration for and adherence to Black capitalism. Although corporations loudly advertised their "participation" in helping Black businesses get on their feet, in truth, these claims were hollow. Whether it was the recession or persistent indifference to the Black struggle, most of these companies offered very little tangible support to Black businesses. In 1970, a *Harvard Business Review* study found that hardly any of the top five hundred corporations or businesses had meaningfully contributed to Black businesses under Nixon's Black capitalism charade. With management unmotivated by the weak incentives offered by the administration, the study's authors reported, "most of the existing efforts by white corporate executives to assist black business came about as a result of fear engendered by the ghetto riots, threats, and pressures from militants, and to some extent pressure of influence from government officials." Much like today's DEI initiatives, these efforts were mainly about corporate marketing rather than tangible justice. Yet without making a dent in terms of real economic progress, they managed to stoke the culture wars and racial backlash that would keep the Right in power for another generation.

Shultz's Philadelphia Plan was neither the result of civil rights groups' advocacy nor a product of altruism from the Nixon administration. Instead, it was a cost-efficient alternative to more redistributive proposals. And the backlash from blue-collar unions over its hiring quotas offered a potential conflict some historians argue was an intentional outcome. Nevertheless, the plan would soon come under fire, most notably from white union workers. Unionized blue-collar workers were among the New Deal Democrats whom the Nixon administration's clever weaponization of race turned into free-market libertarians. Affirmative action was a political sword to cleanly sever the two key Democratic constituencies—blue-collar workers and minorities— from each other, which, according to some historians of the Nixon era, may have been its intended consequence. As John Ehrlichman wrote in his memoirs, "Shultz had shown great style in constructing a political dilemma for the labor leaders and civil rights groups."

Even as Black capitalism offered no genuine economic relief— and very little opportunity for progress—to Black America, Nixon reaped a crucial benefit of its message: Black militants were subdued. While J. Edgar Hoover wielded the FBI mightily against the Black Panthers, imprisoning, accosting, and even murdering members, the Panthers were ultimately brought to an end by dwindling resources and support. White Vietnam War protesters had stood in solidarity with Black activists for a while, but this coalition lost momentum once the war ended. Even more importantly, the feeble gestures toward Black capitalism, such as affirmative action, temporarily placated Black moderates, who slowly withdrew any support they had once extended to the radical movement.

Another crucial source of power for the Black community, collective action, was severely hindered by Black capitalism. Not only did it siphon off at least a few Black businessmen and other members of the Black middle class, aligning them more closely with white America's large business culture; it also drained funds from the remaining War on Poverty programs and stopped potential interracial collective action, which might have arisen from unity under poverty.

The radicalism of the Panthers and the Black Power movement was replaced with a much more moderate and pragmatic approach to Black leadership. The press was quick to catch the Black business craze. *Black Enterprise* launched a publication to illuminate Black businesses, and long-established magazines like *Ebony* and *Jet* dedicated sections to success stories. In the media, *The Jeffersons* used the theme song and slogan "Movin' On Up" to highlight the thesis of the popular show: a Black family "making it" from the ghetto "to the East Side / To a deluxe apartment in the sky," due to the patriarch's keen business prowess.

AMERICA HAD ENTERED A period in which people of all stripes— even white businessmen—were touting the virtues of Black banking and business. Andrew Brimmer's voice, however, rose above the din. Having earned his PhD in economics from Harvard before being appointed the first Black governor of the Federal Reserve by President Johnson, Brimmer possessed a sharp economic mind. "The only really promising path to equal opportunity for Negroes in business as in other aspects of economic activity," he maintained, "lies in full participation in an integrated, national economy. It cannot be found in a backwater of separation and segregation." He went so far as to testify against Black capitalism before the House Committee on Small Business, pointing out that Black families did not have enough capital or income to meaningfully participate in industry. He called out Nixon's Black capitalism as "snake oil."

Brimmer avoided simplistic criticisms of capitalism as inherently exploitative of the Black community, and did not frame Black bankers as exploitative or traitorous to the Black community. Instead, he simply argued that Black banks had too many economic odds stacked against them to manage the task of building wealth in and for Black communities. And research supported his analysis. Black banks still faced the same hurdles: it was difficult to grow capital in a community that had been starved of capital by a legacy of segregation. If the goal was to multiply the Black dollar in hopes of enriching the ghetto economy, this goal was not being met. Black nationalist Reverend Albert Cleage went even further, denouncing not just *Black* capitalism but capitalism: "as far as the black community is concerned, the capitalistic economy doesn't work for us because we don't have any stake in it. It just happens that when we got to a place where we were able to do something, we were outside and the concentration of wealth in the white capitalistic set up is so complete now that you can't break into that . . . we are frozen outside of it."

WITH THE BLACK COMMUNITY having been frozen out, many of the demands for recompense focused on entry into the system. One such avenue of entry was reparations, which Black activists saw as a step toward bridging the gap America had created and widened. But, of course, capitalism itself was thrown up as a counterargument to the need for and justice of reparations. Capitalism, shouted the dissenters, had equal opportunity *built into it.* This circular argument ignored all valid evidence to the contrary.

Alan Greenspan dismissed the demand for reparations in a memo: "The critical question is, of course, whether the Negroes are correct in claiming that they have been exploited and that their violent reaction is the rational response. There can be little doubt that discrimination has been rampant. However, the charge of exploitation in the sense of value being extracted from the Negroes without their consent for the profit of the whites is clearly false. . . . This distinction between discrimination and exploitation is all the difference in the world." Not only did he deny that whites had gained from the losses endured by Black people; he pointed to financial assistance in the ghetto as a threat to the free market. In the end, his advice to Nixon was to "help Negroes help themselves."

In his book *Capitalism and Freedom,* Milton Friedman drew parallels between laws that prohibited discrimination and laws that required it, chalking both up to unhelpful and undesirable government intrusion. He continued this line of thought, reasoning that if left to their own natural processes, markets would disincentivize discrimination. In theory, it was and is true that choosing not to enter into business with sectors of the broader population is inefficient. However, in practice, this logic did not pan out. Whites had, indeed, gained much of their economic foothold precisely through discrimination.

What Friedman and Greenspan were depicting was not the lived reality that had unfurled in America; it was a libertarian fantasy based on theory alone. Americans clung tightly to this neoliberal notion of free-market capitalism, just as they clung to the ideals of liberty and justice for all. These convictions allowed them to reject "government interference" to amend the ills suffered by Black people without a second thought, all in the name of capitalism. Where racial hierarchy and injustice had once been justified by Christianity, then social Darwinism and other bastardizations of science, now it was being propped up by adherence to the principles of capitalist theory. While history clearly showed that Black poverty was a direct result of racist laws and segregation, and the institution of slavery before them, the new neoliberal ideological order claimed that this poverty was the inevitable result of the capitalist machine.

CHAPTER 7

The Free Market Confronts Black Poverty

■   ■   ■   ■   ■   ■   ■

T HE PROMISE OF BLACK CAPITALISM was so politically appealing that every presidential administration since that of Richard Nixon has adopted it in one form or another, be it "community capitalism," "enterprise zones," or "minority enterprise." President Reagan called Black business and Black banking the "key to black economic progress" and promised that Black banks could have a "beneficial multiplier effect" in Black ghettos. President Clinton created robust legislation to promote "community empowerment" through banking—an infrastructure that every administration since has bolstered and maintained. Amid a widening racial wealth gap, the promotion of Black banking and microenterprise has been a consistent policy Band-Aid.

But these "solutions" have turned out to be smoke-screen responses to the fundamental challenge of overcoming America's legacy of slavery and institutional racism. Instead of providing meaningful financial inclusion, key policymakers continue to believe that bankers will save the ghetto. But Black capitalism has not closed the racial wealth gap, because that was not its intent. Nor has Black capitalism lowered racial hostility. Rather, it has stoked white rage and the myth that minorities receive special treatment from the federal government, which has fueled endless cycles of right-wing backlash that have weakened all government benefit programs. That *was* its intent.

Black capitalism and the neoliberal ideology of which it is but one manifestation has enabled the maintenance of a white-dominated economic structure while removing the barriers against capital's perpetual growth. It has beggared us all. While decrying Black communities for mooching off government excess, neoliberal politics has enabled financial firms to loot the coffers of the state. Again and again, racism has been used as a political weapon to divide the people while a group of powerful elites continues to enrich itself. Through various acts of legislation, Black capitalism has grown into a bureaucracy of minority banks, affirmative action, and DEI programs. Yet thanks to a series of Supreme Court decisions, any program meant to benefit minorities—whether affirmative action in admissions or affirmative action in business—cannot be linked to past injustices; rather, it must be justified under the false ideology of a color-blind Constitution.

In a 1978 Supreme Court case addressing the constitutionality of affirmative action, *Bakke v. University of California*, the court ruled that affirmative action was only constitutional as a First Amendment right when used by universities to diversify their student bodies. Although the decision has been heralded as upholding affirmative action, the reasoning of the court effectively neutered any government program aimed at remedying past injustice through said action. Nixon's entire Black capitalism program, including affirmative action, had been premised as a solution—albeit an anemic one—to historic inequalities caused by racist laws and policies. Now the court, led by Nixon appointee and right-wing champion Lewis Powell, barred the government and even private institutions from any program with favorable racial treatment meant to right historic wrongs. Justice Thurgood Marshall, who spent his legal career trying to use the Constitution to remedy past injustice, wrote an impassioned dissent, decrying the court for its decision when so much work remained. "Measured by any benchmark of comfort or achievement," he wrote, "meaningful equality remains a distant dream for the Negro."

Eleven years later, in 1989's *City of Richmond v. J. A. Croson*, the court invalidated a government set-aside program, the main part of Nixon's 1969 Philadelphia Plan, that had required a portion of government contracts be allocated to minority businesses. Writing for a conservative majority, Justice Sandra Day O'Connor used Martin Luther King's words to justify removing initiatives aimed at leveling the racial playing field: "The dream of a Nation of equal citizens in a society where race is irrelevant to personal opportunity and achievement would be lost in a mosaic of shifting preferences based on inherently unmeasurable claims of past wrongs." Despite glaring evidence to the contrary in King's writing and speeches, lawmakers selectively weaponized his rhetoric against affirmative action programs.

The irony is that the Constitution has never been color-blind—it justified slavery, Jim Crow, separate but equal, and other explicitly racist exclusions. But as soon as civil rights laws demanded that it protect all citizens equally, the courts began to take equality literally, demanding that the Constitution not see race at all. Color-blindness, urged by King and the Civil Rights Movement as a path toward justice, became the block preventing the nation from actually addressing its history. The court's decisions amounted to a forced constitutional forgetting of past injustices, forbidding any laws favoring minorities—even as American history was full of laws discriminating against those same minorities.

With the Constitution blocking policy aimed at remedying historic injustice, that historic injustice continued to self-perpetuate, and new ideologies rose up with each successive administration to excuse it.

NOT ONLY WAS THE Constitution's non-color-blind history erased; the history of the civil rights era was rewritten. The fight for Black equality had been a valiant one, with the heroic Martin Luther King Jr. at its helm, and fortunately for all, it had won. King had demanded that the nation stop seeing race, and the nation had heeded his call. Erased from King's legacy, however, was his central point: the nation must acknowledge and *repair* its history of discrimination, which had left the country so unequal. The history of injustice that brought about the fight in the first place, the complexity of King's leadership, and—most of all—the desired outcome of the long fight were all but erased by this facile new narrative. And above all else, this version of the story put the onus of the ongoing disparity on Black people themselves.

President Reagan perhaps did more than anyone to push this color-blind fairy tale. He made King's birthday a national holiday, announcing, "We've made historic strides since Rosa Parks refused to go to the back of the bus. As a democratic people, we can take pride in the knowledge that we Americans recognized a grave injustice and took action to correct it." But Reagan went on to malign "welfare queens" (a term specifically linked to the stereotype of a Black female grifter, despite the fact that most welfare benefits went to whites) for soaking up government handouts at the expense of hardworking taxpayers, a rhetorical turn that couldn't possibly be racist; after all, racism was over! Despite decades of federal assistance that had built and then bolstered the white middle class while pummeling the Black poor, it was now Black mothers who were taking advantage of government largesse. While neoliberal policies unleashed Wall Street's "Age of Greed" through financial deregulation and tax cuts for the wealthy, the Reagan administration weakened unions, cut welfare, lowered the minimum wage, and eliminated pensions. The cuts to the social welfare state were felt by all Americans, not just Black communities. And, having been led to believe that welfare was being abused by Black mothers, those same Americans cheered on the looting by the neoliberal state.

WITH ANY VESTIGIAL LINK between Black capitalism and historic discrimination wiped away by the Supreme Court's rulings, Black businesses became a tokenized stand-in for the broader neoliberal belief that more capitalism was the solution to inequality. Reagan proclaimed that his anti-welfare stance, tax cuts for the rich, and other regressive policies of his "trickle-down" economic theory were all in the name of an "opportunity society" that would benefit Black people as much as whites. He linked his belief in market deregulation with civil rights, declaring, "A free economy helps defeat discrimination by fostering opportunity for all," and he supported minority enterprise, promising that it would "afford socially and economically disadvantaged individuals the opportunity for full participation in our free enterprise system."

But Reagan offered tax cuts instead of solid plans to create either opportunities or jobs for the poor. In place of tangible solutions, he dubbed ghettos "opportunity zones," calling on Congress to "draw a green line of prosperity around the red-lined areas of our cities and to help create jobs and entrepreneurial opportunities." This was Reagan's entire civil rights agenda: tax cuts. The civil rights plank in the 1988 GOP platform promised to "increase, strengthen, and reinvigorate minority business development efforts to afford socially and economically disadvantaged individuals the opportunity for full participation in our free enterprise system." Reagan did not offer any specific plans to create these jobs or opportunities, reasoning that lower taxes and fewer regulations would revitalize the areas and attract more small businesses. The presumption, based on neoliberal dogma, was that unrestrained capitalism would eradicate racial inequality.

In a 1982 speech, Reagan declared that for the rest of his administration, the first week of October would be "Minority Enterprise Development Week." In 1983, he issued an executive order requiring federal agencies to provide annual goals on increasing procurements from minority businesses. All of this was cribbed from right-wing think tanks, such as the Heritage Foundation and the American Enterprise Institute, which rejected fixing the unresolved issue of a historic racial wealth gap in favor of programs that gave the illusion of something being done. And thanks to the Supreme Court's rulings, the minority business programs became a jumble of contradictory motives and legalese.

For example, both President Carter and President Reagan passed initiatives to include women in most of the Small Business Administration and Minority Business Development Agency grant programs. President Reagan's Women's Business Ownership Act of 1988 mandated that the SBA provide additional aid to female-owned enterprise. But the theory of Black enterprise was no longer discussed as an antipoverty measure, and certainly not as a Black Power initiative. Instead, it was framed as a set of positive role models for minority communities and efforts to "diversify" white-male dominated fields. With so much legal and political attention paid to breaking into the margins of the white-dominated economic structure, the structure itself was allowed to remain intact. Allowed, in fact, to grow into a predatory financial behemoth.

REAGAN'S SIGNATURE PROGRAMS DEALING with the segregated Black ghettos were the War on Crime and the War on Drugs, which together led to the mass incarceration of millions of Black men. Here, he was picking up on and expanding the Nixon administration's law-and-order rhetoric that linked Black communities with criminality. The dual wars—on drugs and crime—were, in fact, a war on Black communities. They boosted federal investment in law enforcement (while drying up investment in drug-abuse and use-prevention programs), created a system in which Black sentences were much more stringent than white sentences, and—most crucially—did deep, complex damage to generations of young Black men.

The War on Drugs and the War on Crime were not waged in response to a rise in drug use and crime—though the heavy policing, cuts in welfare, and harsh prison sentences demanded by these policies exacerbated the socioeconomic dynamics that led to such a rise. Rather, the rhetoric of blame toward the Black community for the nation's problems was a continuation of the Nixonian Southern strategy. A long-serving Republican adviser and Nixon's top aide, John Ehrlichman, revealed the playbook in a 1994 interview. "You want to know what this was really all about?" said Ehrlichman. "The Nixon campaign in 1968, and the Nixon White House after that, had two enemies: the antiwar left and black people. . . . We knew we couldn't make it illegal to be either against the war or black, but by getting the public to associate the hippies with marijuana and blacks with heroin, and then criminalizing both heavily, we could disrupt those communities. We could arrest their leaders, raid their homes, break up their meetings, and vilify them night after night on the evening news. Did we know we were lying about the drugs? Of course we did."

Lifetime sentences were readily doled out for crack users and distributors in the ghetto, purportedly to disband the crack "epidemic" unfolding there. When the War on Drugs began, inner-city crack use hardly qualified as an epidemic. But media attention, law enforcement intervention, and harsh punishments, coupled with poverty, soon made it one. And the national preoccupation with crack quickly displaced any focus on structural poverty. Poverty, segregation, and heavy policing in the ghetto had a magnifying effect on drug use, gang violence, and other crimes, which bloomed into serious problems for the already-marginalized urban poor. Adam Walinsky, Senator Robert F. Kennedy's speechwriter, explained this phenomenon succinctly: "If we blame crime on crack, our politicians are off the hook. Forgotten are the failed schools, the maligned welfare programs, the desolate neighborhoods, the wasted years. Only crack is to blame. One is tempted to think that if crack did not exist, someone somewhere would have received a Federal grant to develop it." In fact, as with the Minority Enterprise agenda, the rhetoric of the War on Drugs and the War on Crime and the policies themselves were spawned in right-wing circles like the Heritage Foundation's *Mandate for Leadership* book series, which shaped much of Reagan's policy agenda.

Politicians saw the opportunity in white fear and zeroed in on the political affordances of "tough on crime" rhetoric. On the campaign trail, George H. W. Bush forged a link between his opponent, Michael Dukakis, and Willie Horton, who had committed a rape and a robbery after being released during Dukakis's governorship. Bill

Clinton took a more macabre approach. He left the campaign trail to oversee the execution of Ricky Ray Rector, a mentally incapacitated Black man who had killed a police officer. Both Bush and Clinton won the presidency.

The War on Crime burgeoned under the Clinton administration. Incarcerations skyrocketed, federal support for welfare and public housing was cut, and a "One Strike and You're Out" public housing policy yielded countless evictions for trivial offenses. Yet Clinton blamed the Black community for its "downward spiral." Standing on the site of King's historic "I've Been to the Mountaintop" speech, the president lambasted his audience:

> If [Martin Luther King] were to reappear by my side today and give us a report card on the last 25 years, what would he say? . . . "You did a good job," he would say, "letting people who have the ability to do so live wherever they want to live, go wherever they want in this great country." . . . But he would say, "I did not live and die to see the American family destroyed. . . . I did not fight for the right of black people to murder other black people with reckless abandon."

Despite Clinton's hollow celebration of integration, the government had long abandoned any real initiatives to combat segregation. By the end of Clinton's time in the White House, eight hundred thousand Black men were in prison (while only six hundred thousand were in college). Ex-felons were disenfranchised and unemployable—meaning an inevitable return to the ghetto. Clinton slashed welfare benefits, which he believed caused a cycle of dependence. Calling himself a "New Democrat," he proposed a "third way" platform between Republicans and Democrats, but that third way was essentially more neoliberalism and more Black capitalism.

Clinton's urban poverty programs were firmly embedded in neoliberal market ideology—the market would fix racial injustice and make a profit doing so! The country's racial ghettos, whose walls remained intact, came to be referred to as enterprise zones, emerging markets, and niche industries. Clinton passed a series of laws with tax inducements to encourage private firms to invest in these impoverished communities. These areas could yield a profit—if creative entrepreneurs only looked hard enough. Essentially, Clinton's policies provided an incentive-based boost to Nixon's Black capitalism framework. Nixon had tried—with minimal effort and minimal success—to induce large white-owned firms to *voluntarily* contribute to Black businesses. Even the firms themselves had viewed their involvement as charitable and entirely voluntary.

In contrast, Clinton's program did not appeal to philanthropic aims. He promised profits. His Department of Housing and Urban Development (HUD) secretary, Andrew Cuomo, told reporters, "[It] is not about charity. It's about investment." Instead of working to break down the walls of segregation and the poverty trap, academics and progressive reformers agreed that ghetto poverty was a result of misaligned market incentives, which could only be addressed through private enterprise. As the influential Harvard professor Michael Porter wrote, the only way to build the economy of the ghetto was "through private, for-profit initiatives and investment based on economic self-interest and genuine advantage. . . . The cornerstone of such a model is to identify and exploit the competitive advantages of inner cities that will translate into truly profitable businesses." This rhetoric emphasized a win-win of profits for the entrepreneurs and poverty alleviation for the ghetto.

Because the Supreme Court had found remedying past wrongs to be unconstitutional, an era of so-called color-blindness had ensued. Any programs directed toward the country's ghettos had to be race-neutral, and so Black capitalism became "community capitalism." A 1997 conference, the American Assembly, brought together business and community leaders and academics to discuss poverty and community development. The final conference report defined community capitalism as a "for-profit, business-driven expansion of investment, job creation, and economic opportunities in distressed communities, with government and the community sectors playing key supportive roles." Vice President Al Gore endorsed the report, stating, "The greatest untapped markets in the world are right here at home, in our distressed communities."

CLINTON'S "COMMUNITY CAPITALISM" PROGRAM, as applied to banks, was the Riegle Community Development and Regulatory Improvement Act of 1994, commonly known as the Community Development Banking Act. The act provided tax incentives for banks, or community development financial institutions (CDFIs), that served disadvantaged areas. According to Clinton, the ShoreBank on Chicago's South Side, which was putting the theory of community capitalism into practice, inspired the bill. The bank's ambitious mission drew many admirers, including Grameen Bank founder Muhammad Yunus, who visited the bank before launching microcredit in Bangladesh and receiving a Nobel Peace Prize for his innovative approach to poverty. Deeply embedded in neoliberal economics, the promise of microcredit and CDFIs was that self-help remedies like small lending could over-come entrenched historic inequalities.

In promoting the ShoreBank model, Clinton outlined his early vision for community empowerment:

> You have to go into these areas with strategies that enable people to take control of their own destiny. . . . We need to create a small-business entrepreneurial economy in every underclass urban area and rural area in the country through the use of banks like the South Shore Bank, which played a major role in revitalizing the South Side of Chicago. . . . Trying to create an entrepreneurial economy around a different sort of banking system . . . would make a real difference.

This "different sort of banking system" of small community banks, however, operated only in poor minority communities. For the main-stream banking system, the Clinton administration continued the massive Wall Street deregulation begun by President Reagan. In fact, Clinton and his treasury secretaries, former Goldman Sachs partner Robert Rubin and his successor, Larry Summers, went even further than Reagan by passing the Gramm-Leach-Bliley Act, which over-turned the bank safety protections passed under the New Deal–era Glass-Steagall Act. The combined effect of these laws was indeed a different kind of banking system, one that would grow larger, more concentrated, riskier, and much more profitable than our nation had ever seen. A different sort of economy arose, too, as finance became a central force. Unrestrained by law, balance sheets grew at an unprecedented rate in the coffers of these newly formed banking conglomerates.

Bank assets are, in fact, people's debts. And banks make profits from interest rates. Thus, the growth of bank profits correlated precisely with the nation's mounting debts. Credit card, mortgage, and business debt fed capital's hunger for more yield, but so, too, did sovereign debt—until the entire global market was sucked into the centripetal force of the nation's growing banking conglomerates. In search of ever more yield, Wall Street would create a massive subprime mortgage market, which would soon come to the nation's formerly redlined areas. Clinton and Summers were right: there were profits to be made in distressed communities; only those profits would come at a great expense to the communities themselves.

Clinton was just the latest American leader to sell out Black people so that the moneyed interests could have their way with the country. The trick, then and now, was that to sell out Black people, you had to throw all poor people into the financial industry's wood chipper. A bipartisan consensus of neoliberal lawmakers enabled the looting of the nation by global financial firms while blaming Black people for rising crime. Not for the first time in history, the scapegoating of Black people for violence, lawlessness, and bad moral character shielded the financial-legal industrial complex (the white guys in suits) from the consequences of their actions.

Even as the Reagan and Clinton administrations blamed Black communities' bad decision-making for their poverty, they created laws enabling unprecedent recklessness on Wall Street. As Black families were being admonished for overspending, Wall Street balance sheets were pushing the boundaries of leverage and debt. While the Right blamed welfare and handouts for the federal deficit, the Federal Reserve was advancing trillions of dollars of credit to the nation's top banks. When the banks failed in 2008, it became clear that the myths of the neoliberal era—that the free market could manage itself without government input and deliver widespread equality—had failed, too. The "market," it turned out, was an extension of the state. Its recovery hinged exactly on how much money the Federal Reserve was willing to print to save it. That number, it turned out, was trillions more than the government was willing to spend on remedying America's long history of entrenched racial injustice.

The market the state saved had not delivered shared prosperity. It had concentrated wealth at the top—wealth that would only grow after the financial crisis. In fact, the crisis hardly disabused policymakers of their guiding neoliberal dogmas. Instead, it reinforced racial tropes of Black incompetence, blaming poor Black Americans for buying homes they could not afford.

The disproportionate impact of the 2008 financial crisis on Black Americans can be attributed directly to segregation. The crisis eradicated 53 percent of total Black wealth. It was, as former North Carolina Representative Brad Miller called it, an "extinction event" that precipitated staggering losses in the Black community. Over 240,000 Black families lost their homes, and 35 percent ended up with zero or negative wealth. One of the most significant reasons was subprime mortgage lending. With tragic predictability, however, conservatives were quick to point the finger at DEI and affirmative action programs and critique the "reverse racism" of policies that encouraged and supported lending to minorities. Even more upsettingly, the result of this fallacious rhetoric was that the bottom-line blame rested on the shoulders of the borrowers. As Rick Santelli infamously hollered (in a speech that has been considered the genesis of the Tea Party movement), "How many of you people want to pay for your neighbor's mortgage that has an extra bathroom and can't pay their bills?" Unsurprisingly, Tea Party ideology was laced with racial animosity and neatly incorporated Gold-water and Nixon's stereotype of Black "freeloaders."

The example of Clinton's celebrated ShoreBank is telling—and recalls, too, the Binga State Bank of the early twentieth century. While Wall Street received upwards of a trillion dollars in bailout funds, it was ShoreBank's application for $70 million in bailout funds that created a media firestorm; that rage was not only disproportionate to the funds requested but completely disconnected to the scale of the total bank bailout. The unprecedented scrutiny and attention directed at ShoreBank's failure matched the hubbub over its founding—the press couldn't resist reporting on the demise of Clinton and Obama's favorite bank and calling out "political favoritism." Glenn Beck used his famous chalkboard to weave a ludicrous conspiracy theory that connected ShoreBank to all his favorite enemies, including President Obama, ACORN, Bill Ayers, and Hillary Clinton. In the end, Shore-Bank did not receive a bailout and failed, causing losses to inner-city Chicago residents and bank investors. The bank's assets were taken over by Urban Partnership Bank, a consortium of top Wall Street Banks and investors, including Goldman Sachs, American Express, Citigroup, Bank of America, JPMorgan Chase, GE Capital, Morgan Stanley, and Wells Fargo, all of whom had received not millions but billions in bailout funds.

As the previous chapters have shown, decades of government-sponsored redlining had created a massive wealth gap that cordoned off America's riskiest borrowers in segregated Black neighborhoods. Instead of dealing with this racial wealth gap through government policy, both Democratic and Republican administrations criminalized poverty and deified the market. Market magic, said Reagan, would lead to shared prosperity and equality for all. The era of Wall Street greed coincided with an era in which the walls separating money and politics were also deregulated. Increasingly, Wall Street and Washington spoke with the same voice. Black communities had been sacrificed to the demands of the cotton empire during the sharecropping era. Now they were sacrificed once again to the demands of the predatory mortgage market.

As capital grew, it became more usurious. Usury laws, which had kept interest rates capped at 6 percent, were deregulated in 1978 in a decision written by neoliberal Supreme Court Justice Lewis Powell, and the race to the bottom was on. With lenders now able to charge interest rates upwards of 500 percent APR on small loans, 36 percent on credit cards, and 15 percent on subprime loans, the riskiest borrowers became a source of profits for Wall Street's usurious financial engine. And when that engine sputtered out, having overgorged itself on risk, the Washington–Wall Street elites saved it, some of them cynically blaming Black people once again.

WHEN THE FINANCIAL CRISIS Inquiry Commission released its definitive report on the subprime mortgage crisis, it determined that the failures had essentially been caused by banks taking too much risk in the pursuit of profit. But commission member Peter Wallison, a senior fellow at the American Enterprise Institute, dissented. He blamed the financial crisis on government policies like the Community Reinvestment Act (CRA), which promoted lending to minorities. Wallison's claim was that government policies forced banks to lend to minority communities, thereby weakening them, a theory parroted by politicians, pundits, and academics.

The CRA was affirmative action in lending. Although it was

designed to remedy racially explicit redlining, which had calcified segregation patterns and exacerbated the racial wealth gap, it could only
offer a color-blind remedy. The CRA asked banks to "diversify" their
portfolios by offering some loans in underserved areas. Like affirmative
action, the services the banks provided in these areas were treated as a
sideshow—the main event being the bank's normal, profitable business
of lending into the white-dominated economic structure. Much like
affirmative action, the CRA did nothing to shake the foundations of
an economic system built on racial discrimination.

Yet, also like affirmative action, the CRA has been one of the most
vilified banking laws, even as civil rights groups criticized its "toothless" efforts to counteract the legacy of past injustices. Republican
members of the House blamed the CRA for the financial crisis, stating, "For years Congress has been pushing banks to make risky subprime loans. . . . Congress passed laws that said we're going to fine you
and we're going to file lawsuits against you lenders if you don't make
risky loans." A Fox News commentator remarked, "Look . . . you go
all the way back to the Community Reinvestment Act, under Jimmy
Carter, expanded under Bill and Hillary Clinton—they put the guns
to the banks' heads, and said, 'You have got to do these subprime
loans.' . . . That's what caused this mess."

Blaming the CRA and reckless government policies became code
for lending to minorities. The moral outrage was directed at the borrowers, not the banks. Rick Santelli's infamous rant on the Chicago
trading floor was a diatribe against the injustice of hardworking Americans paying for frivolous and irresponsible debtors that bought homes
they could not afford. He denounced them as "losers." This sort of
resentment, which bore more than a hint of racial animosity, resonated
with many. Research showed that the Tea Party movement, ostensibly

about government overreach, was directly correlated with a racist backlash. This is consistent with the neoliberal message associating government largesse with Black freeloaders.

The theory that the CRA or government mortgage policy in any way led to the financial crisis has been debunked by scholars, as well as by influential policymakers like the Federal Reserve chair and the treasury secretary. Every serious analysis has concluded that the CRA did not cause the rise in subprime lending. How could it? The act was passed in 1977; subprime lending started heating up more than twenty years later. The majority of the crisis-causing subprime loans were not given out by lenders with any CRA obligations—only 6 percent of subprime loans were even CRA loans. Yet pundits and politicians continue to blame the one law aimed at increasing minority lending for the entire financial crisis. Like President Reagan's invocation of "welfare queens," this narrative paints low-income subprime borrowers as irresponsible exploiters of taxpayer money and government benevolence. In fact, the banks wanted subprime loans because they were making unprecedented profits. Subprime lenders popped up in ghettos not because the government or community activists wanted them there but because that was where they could convince more people to take out subprime loans.

Neoliberalism in financial law translated to an unfettered capital market whose voracious hunger for yield demanded debt contracts at an unprecedented scale. As capital on bank balance sheets grew to the trillions, capital's shadow, debt, fed that growth. Wall Street went looking for new forms of risk to feed into the yield-producing machine. Yield is another way of saying risk; for capital to grow through yield, it needs new markets of risk and debt to exploit.

Wall Street found these new markets in the segregated ghettos. They were more than encouraged by the neoliberal financial agencies of the Reagan, Clinton, and Bush eras, whose answer to racial inequality was: more capitalism.

Wall Street also lobbied for government policy and programs to drop standards for underwriting. Risky ghetto borrowers with sparse credit histories—also known as "thin file" credit—became easy prey for investors seeking untapped profits. The subprime market was so profitable that banks began giving subprime loans even when borrowers could have qualified for better ones—especially when the borrower was Black. As the Center for Responsible Lending discovered, Black borrowers were 150 percent more likely than their white counterparts to be issued a subprime loan. Companies like Countrywide specifically targeted inner cities; many areas marked as focal points had been redlined districts.

Those who blame the CRA for the crisis assume that it is an aberrant government intrusion into an efficient market order. Much like with affirmative action, there is a perceived feeling that institutions are being forced to admit lower-quality students or make lower-quality loans to appease some vague sense of social morality. Detractors of affirmative action argue that schools should select students only on the basis of academic merit. Similarly, banks should lend only with an eye toward profitability. When the CRA was introduced, the bill was strongly condemned by many bankers and their allies. Republican Senator Phil Gramm called the act "an evil like slavery in the pre–Civil War era." "It's unbelievable," fumed one anonymous Southern banker. "These people are trying to enforce a change in social policy over the back of the banking industry." At the core of their argument was the claim that the CRA conflicted with natural meritocracy or an efficient market. Here again, a status quo caused by centuries of discrimination was taken as "natural" and "neutral"—rather than a creation of law and policy—and any programs aimed at inclusion were an unnatural, harmful "intervention."

Opponents of affirmative action similarly claim that the policy harms both the school and the minority applicant. They reason that the minority applicants perform more poorly than the white ones and that when underperforming minority students gain admission, there is a "mismatch" of capacity. According to this widely cited "mismatch theory," whites should continue to fill elite universities until Black students catch up naturally. The anti-CRA messaging follows a similar line of logic by claiming that banks should avoid lending into distressed areas. Residents of these areas are more likely to default on a loan, because they have fewer resources. The banks are not discriminating; they are avoiding nonprofitable areas and riskier loans. Applying the mismatch theory to banking results in the notion that borrowers should work to earn bank loans instead of being offered the loans prematurely.

But these arguments only touch on surface-level problems and fail to explore why Black students and Black borrowers lag behind whites in the first place. A history of segregation explains why the ghetto does not yield profitable loans. More specifically, segregation was enacted through lending discrimination perpetuated by the very firms now being asked to close the gap. That still unremedied history of segregation and the pockets of concentrated poverty it produced made Black communities the targets of the worst of Wall Street's subprime loans. Mortgage loan rates were significantly higher for Black borrowers than for white ones, and repayment periods were longer. This disparity remained even when income and other factors held steady—lenders targeted Black borrowers with their most costly loans. One massive Federal Reserve study, which looked at 6.4 million mortgage applications, found pervasive institutionalized discrimination based on race in the banking sector. A HUD study determined that "high-cost subprime lending accounted for 51 percent of home loans" in Black neighborhoods, whereas it only made up 9 percent of the figure in white neighborhoods. The study also found that "homeowners in high-income black neighborhoods [were] twice as likely as homeowners in low-income white neighborhoods to have subprime loans." In many of these studies, the borrower's race was noted as a key factor in determining interest rates.

But the disparity had a deeper and more intricate root system. Though the lending market was indeed permeated by racism, there was also the cold, hard truth that due to a long history of exclusion and exploitation, Black communities had less wealth than white communities, which made them riskier borrowers. Both elements combined to ensnare Black borrowers—even those that were creditworthy—in the imbalanced system. And since mortgage lenders had figured out that they actually benefited from extending these more expensive loans to credit-compromised ghetto residents, they inundated the ghetto. Donald Riegle, a Michigan senator, referred to the practice as "reverse redlining." "This is a system of segregation, really," stated one attorney. "We don't have separate water fountains, but we have separate lending institutions."

THE VILIFICATION OF IRRESPONSIBLE Black communities and the government largesse that enabled them allowed for another historic transfer of wealth: the federal government providing bankers and bank shareholders with trillions of dollars in government bailouts and Federal Reserve "rescue" programs. Only a minuscule amount of these trillions went to actually saving homeowners from the catastrophic losses caused by Wall Street's risk-taking. Rather than bail out irresponsible people from their bad decisions—according to the mainstream narrative—the banks received trillions in public money, despite the irresponsible decisions they, too, had made.

Although the bank bailouts began during the Bush administration (with an admittedly confused president deferring all decisions to his treasury secretary, former Goldman Sachs CEO Hank Paulson), it was up to President Obama to sell them to the public. Obama also deferred to his top economic adviser, Larry Summers. Having led the neoliberal transition under Clinton, Summers was focused primarily on saving his legacy and the integrity of the financial behemoth he had helped build. And so Obama, the first Black president, whose campaign speeches on the economy evoked FDR, stepped up to save the banks from the wrath of the people. He was left with no choice but to politely ask AIG executives to forgo millions of dollars in bonuses, which the firm paid out despite having received billions in government bailouts. "I am standing between you and the pitchforks," he warned the executives, but his pleas failed to persuade even his own economic advisers, who argued that the banks had to deliver the bonuses or risk breaching their executives' contracts.

As for the social contract, the promises he had made to voters, and the "pitchforks"? Obama was silent. Perhaps confused by the impenetrable financial mumbo jumbo experts like Larry Summers threw at him about "risk management" and "stress testing," the "Hope and Change" president was persuaded to turn on the big money hose at the Fed and pour it over Wall Street, instead of on the poor and Black people of America. Thus the financial crisis, instead of the natural reset of wealth it could have been, only accelerated the widening racial wealth gap.

Today it is much bigger than a *racial* wealth gap. It is now just a massive wealth gap, with the vast majority of humans on one side of the chasm (the proverbial 99 percent) and a handful of the most corrupt lawmakers and bankers on the other side (the ever-shrinking 1 percent). As the wealthy escape even the confines of democratic participation through taxation, flitting off to their tax shelters and yachts, they continue to claim that their spoils were gained through a fair and free market, to blame Black people for not being good at capitalism, and to promise that the rest of us have a shot at joining them if we just pour more and more of our lives into the usurious and perpetually hungry maw of the modern American economy.

The only fight left to the voters is over DEI—Black capitalism— with one side claiming that it is responsible for the unfairness that exists today and the other claiming that diversifying the cannibalistic financial system will make it fairer. That culture war has enough fuel, thanks to centuries of unremedied racial lies, that it can distract us in election cycle after election cycle, leading millions of voters to ignore the looting occurring right before their eyes—a looting not just of Black America but of all Americans. A looting that began at the very founding of our nation, when instead of fighting for true equality, our founding documents compromised with people's lives—that initial hypocrisy of slavery in the land of the free.

This truth can no longer be ignored. It is the lie that gave birth to "a crippled nation," in King's telling. It is the gap between the law and justice that must be closed. When King said, "Injustice anywhere is a threat to justice everywhere," he was speaking not metaphorically but literally. All of our justice is threatened because we have refused to grant justice to Black people. And that injustice has only grown, as have the lies that uphold it. As I concluded in *The Quiet Coup*, my book about the neoliberal looting of America, justice is not a cost-benefit equation or an efficient analysis, as our current legal system presumes. Justice is a gut feeling. And it is one we all share. We may not know exactly how the rules of the game are rigged, but many can sense that the playing field is not even, that our economy is not totally fair, and that the connection between effort and reward has grown increasingly tenuous. Though the imbalance of the system is widely felt, some have been duped into believing that it is the poor people looting the money, rather than the rich. This misbelief sits alongside racism, which has played such an important role in creating our current confusion.

The 2008 financial crisis and its aftermath were the latest iteration of the old historic pattern: Black poverty plundered by an extractive financial system for its gains, government largesse protecting the property rights and gains of elites, and a subsequent backlash blaming the impoverished Black communities not only for remaining poor but also, unironically, for being the actual recipients of special treatment from the government. It was in the aftermath of the massive bank bailouts and the devastation wrought on the Black community that Donald Trump entered the political scene by accusing President Obama of not being a real American. President Trump rode the political backlash begun by the Tea Party, which laid America's problems at the feet, once again, of minorities. In his second term, he has already coupled extraordinary tax cuts for the rich and further deregulation of Wall Street with an attack on the DEI bureaucracy, which is, in his administration's view, the cause of the unfairness in American society. It is unclear what will happen next, but the scapegoating has begun. As has the perpetual exploitation of average Americans that the cheap political tool of racism has always enabled.

EPILOGUE
Toward Fundamental Reform

■　　■　　■　　■　　■　　■　　■

Aᴅᴅʀᴇssɪɴɢ ᴀɴ ᴀᴜᴅɪᴇɴᴄᴇ ᴏꜰ 250,000 people at the 1963 March on Washington, Martin Luther King Jr. spoke of the "promissory note to which every American was to fall heir. . . . A promise that all men . . . would be guaranteed the unalienable rights of life, liberty, and the pursuit of happiness," as pledged by the government in the Constitution. And yet, he observed, "America has defaulted on this promissory note insofar as her citizens of color are concerned. Instead of honoring this sacred obligation, America has given the Negro people a bad check . . . which has come back marked 'insufficient funds.'" To this day, the breach of contract between the American government and the country's Black citizens remains unresolved.

Iɴ ᴀ ᴄᴏᴜʀᴛ ᴏꜰ ʟᴀᴡ, harm incurred as a result of the violation of a contract is redressed through damages. And Black Americans have long since called for damages from the government in the form of reparations. These calls have not only gone unheeded; they are often countered by the argument that the Constitution precludes the government from using race as a target for compensation, due to its promise of equal treatment. There is brutal irony in this argument, though, since Black communities have suffered for centuries as a *direct result* of the Constitution's own unequal treatment. There also exists a strong counterargument that the Constitution not only allows for but *demands* redress. In 1948, W.E.B. Du Bois announced that the biggest issue with American democracy was that "it ha[s] not yet been tried." Perhaps, today, it is finally time to try.

In place of meaningful recompense for the obvious damage slavery and the subsequent reign of Jim Crow inflicted on the Black community, the American government has proposed self-help solutions. The grossly incorrect assumption undergirding this approach is that the wealth gap, which was created and worsened by poor public policy, can be mended by private markets. As we have seen, Nixon's version of this notion, "Black capitalism," which featured a mostly rhetorical promotion of Black banks and businesses, has been adopted and rebranded by every president since. As a result, the wealth gap has continued to grow.

The effects of the segregated debt market can still be felt today. They have created two separate and unequal systems of banking and credit: the regulated, heavily subsidized mainstream banking industry and the unregulated, costly, and often predatory fringe industry. Having been left out of the former, the Black community has historically occupied the latter—at great expense. On average, a Black customer will pay $425 more than a white customer will for consumer loans. Black neighborhoods are largely "banking deserts," resulting in 60 percent of the Black population being underbanked or entirely unbanked. During the financial crisis in 2008, 93 percent of all banks that closed were in minority areas. And wherever banks depart, loan sharks stream in.

Another unfortunate by-product of banking deserts is the increased need for payday loans. Indeed, Black people are twice as likely as members of any other race to rely on these loans, and debt collectors are five times more likely to be litigious against them. These statistics hold even without overt discrimination, as white communities tend to have a more robust safety net than do Black communities. With such costly credit options, it makes sense that debt collectors extract as many as *five times more* judgments against Black neighborhoods than white ones. Specifically, debt collectors sued one in four Black residents in the studied communities. Most of the other lawsuits were similar: large debt collectors suing for small amounts.

Wealth provides a buffer against the inevitable setbacks and struggles of life. On the flip side, lack of wealth begets such setbacks and struggles. Impoverished Black Americans often face bankruptcy, eviction, legal action, wage garnishment, and other traumatic financial repercussions, thickening what one study referred to as the "web of indebtedness." All of these economic roadblocks are exacerbated and accompanied by other ramifications, such as school closures, high unemployment rates, and calamitous incarceration rates.

The racial wealth gap is large at every income level, and a full third of Black families have no assets whatsoever. Even more disturbing is the fact that studies indicate that the divide is accelerating. This should not be surprising, given the velocity with which capital has been enabled to grow since the neoliberal deregulatory era, coupled with the legal ban on remedying historic discrimination because of a color-blind reading of the Constitution advanced by the Supreme Court in the 1970s and 1980s. Within this racial wealth gap, the injustices of America's past metastasize into the present. Strictures placed on Black business decades ago continue to constrict the Black community, further curtailing the accumulation of wealth. Poverty rates continue to be staggering; 75 percent of Black children born into the bottom tier of wealth remain there into adulthood. Every dollar earned by a white family precipitates an average of $5.19 in wealth, whereas that same dollar yields a mere sixty-nine cents in wealth for Black families. While the removal of explicit racial bans have allowed stellar Black individuals to achieve stardom in every conceivable field and success in every office—including the presidency—most Black Americans remain mired in the still-segregated topography of this nation's economy, where mostly Black and brown neighborhoods are cut off from opportunity for advancement. And now, thanks to decades of neoliberal policymaking and the financial greed it enabled, many all-white towns across the Rust Belt, the rural South, Appalachia, and the Intermountain West have also seen capital flight and the whirlpool of economic decline.

The myth that the wealth gap yawned open as a natural by-product of capitalist market forces still clouds the American ethos today. With it comes the tendency to blame poor Black people for their poverty. But a survey of America's economic history shows the true story: wealth is generational, and so is poverty. Not only does wealth itself get passed down; the trappings that come with affluence make their way from one generation to the next. Among these advantages are higher income, lower incarceration rates, and better education.

Theories about why a significant number of Black Americans remain in poverty abound, echoing with centuries-old justifications of white supremacy. In their 1994 book *The Bell Curve*, Charles Murray and Richard Herrnstein proposed fundamental biological differences between races. Different iterations of this argument imply that Black poverty can be traced to a refusal to work or to take education seriously. Just as biological research indicates that there exist no marked differences along racial lines, economic studies reveal that an upbringing with wealth is the most salient determinant in career and education. Predictably, people with greater wealth receive better educations and thus get higher-paying jobs, reinforcing their access to greater wealth and sustaining the wealth gap.

Another alarmingly prevalent "theory" to explain Black poverty is that the Black community is rife with broken families and lacks "family values." This theory is neither new nor accurate. It was first proposed by Daniel Patrick Moynihan to justify the government's benign neglect of the Black community and has been a favorite talking point of policymakers, who want to justify doing nothing rather than working to alleviate Black poverty. Again, economic research indicates that wealth is a much stronger determinant of family stability in white and Black families alike. Recent studies have unearthed deep psychological ramifications of poverty. Psychological trauma—especially in children—has been traced to extended periods of scarcity, homelessness, and fear, among other factors. These poverty-precipitated conditions lead to decreased social and academic proficiency. Childhood poverty is a trauma that this nation continues to impose on children of all races. In America today, one in every ten white children is raised in poverty; one in every three Black children grows up poor.

Despite mounting evidence compiled through modern research, policymakers approach poverty as the by-product of bad individual choices rather than circumstance. Contrary to the belief that the poor are simply "bad with money" or in need of financial education, studies have shown that poor people tend to be much more careful with their finances than wealthy people. The issue is not spending habits but, rather, access to wealth. Yet initiatives to address the issue remain tied to fruitless efforts to increase financial literacy. In response to a request in 2016 from the president of *Black Enterprise* magazine to address the racial wealth gap, Treasury Secretary Jack Lew pontificated: "Most people buy a cup of coffee without thinking about it. Most people buy an extra magazine or a video without thinking about it. . . . If you take the accumulated decisions people make lightly and in one of those occasions say, 'I am going to put money away for retirement,' you'd see people start out with more. . . . I think financial education, financial literacy is about understanding that some people buying a home might not be a good idea." The baseless notion that Black people would achieve wealth if they improved their money management is alive and well. Again, here, research suggests otherwise. Data show that when controlling for income, Black families save 11 percent of their annual income, as compared to 10 percent savings for whites.

Segregation, too, remains largely unchallenged. There has been no federal integration initiative since George Romney's Open Communities program, despite the fact that the parts of the country with the fewest resources are usually also the ones with the most concentrated Black populations. One of the most problematic by-products of housing segregation is that over time, without federal mandates to oppose the phenomenon, American schools have resegregated. Though rising inequality has depleted the American middle class, the white middle class fares significantly better than does the Black middle class; white families earning $40,000 a year tend to live in wealthier neighborhoods than do Black families earning nearly double that figure, and homes in majority-Black neighborhoods are valued at 23 percent less than those in neighborhoods with very few or no Black residents, even when accounting for factors like neighborhood amenities and housing quality. In the words of Ta-Nehisi Coates, "Poor black people do not

work their way out of the ghetto—and those who do often face the horror of watching their children and grandchildren tumble back."

According to a study conducted in 2016, it would take 228 years
for white and Black Americans to possess equal wealth, extrapolating
from the wealth gap at that time. But this prediction left out the fact
that the wealth gap will *never* close if America's systems continue to
function as they currently do.

A FAR MORE PROMISING way to look at the estimate is to consider that new, fresh ideas could draw the gap closed in a much more
hopeful span of time. A London paper from 1894 predicted that,
judging by current conditions, "Every street in London will be buried
under nine feet of manure" within fifty years. What this estimate did
not—and could not—consider was that the invention of the automo-
bile was already on the horizon. Soon horses would no longer be the
primary mode of transportation. With the right ideas, informed by
a thorough understanding of America's long legacy of injustice, we
need not wait 228 years.

America has a long way to go before it reaches post-racial status.
Still, it is valuable to reflect on the significant and remarkable progress
that *has* been made in so many arenas. Polling about interracial marriage, for instance, reveals an 83 percent approval increase from 1958 to
2013. Though he was not able to bring about the racial harmony many
Americans hoped for, the majority of the country voted to secure the
presidency for Barack Obama—twice. The Human Genome Project
has disbanded the long-held and erroneous notion that race is a meaningful genetic trait. Indeed, race has never been a biological fact, only
a political weapon, and that knowledge has already begun to change
hearts and minds. We have made strides in recognizing the humanity

of others, which only improves our own humanity. Slavery was possible for so long because whites refused to acknowledge the humanity of their Black slaves. In earlier eras, whites could push Black people and other immigrants into ghettos and ignore the disease, squalor, and poverty that resulted—sometimes even using the inevitable decrepitude of the ghetto to justify further dehumanization of minorities. As a society, we can no longer tolerate this—if only because our digital interconnectedness means we can no longer ignore the suffering of others. When images surface of white police officers killing unarmed Black men, the world sees it immediately, and the injustice is difficult to ignore. Slowly but surely, we are taking steps forward.

It can be difficult to see that we are on the path to a more just and equitable future. Police brutality against Black people, hate crimes, racist internet content, and other flagrant exceptions to this steady progression come to mind quickly, and, understandably, they tend to cloud the vision with their darkness. These issues must be contended with and eliminated, of course, but they do not compose the full picture.

If the racial wealth gap is ever to be bridged, and if the deep wounds it has created in Americans of all races are to be healed, a profound understanding of the wealth gap's history—political, social, and economic—must be reached. It is imperative that America face the racist public policy that lies at the very core of the gap. Justice cannot be achieved without recognition of the breach in contract between the American government and its Black citizens—a breach that began when Africans were brought to this continent as slaves, and that has not been remedied since. By its letter, the Constitution prevents both harm and help based on group characteristics, but that very pillar has been violated by the historic treatment of Black Americans. America is long overdue for a full-throated apology for and a reckoning with

all it has done to its Black population. Moreover, there is strong economic backing to the adage "A rising tide lifts all boats." An economy
that grapples with inequity promises economic advancement to all. In
other words, any policy aimed at closing the racial wealth gap will be a
boon to the broader economy—and will go a long way toward closing
the non-racial wealth gap, which has also been growing to unprecedented extremes.

OPPONENTS OF REPARATIONS ABOUND, and their arguments
often involve the notion that such policy is "impractical." But the prec-
edent for reparations has been established by the courts throughout
history. In recent years, America's courts have extracted hundreds of
billions of dollars in damages from oil companies, opioid drug manu-
facturers, and tobacco companies. Just as the victims of environmental damage, unwitting drug addiction and overdose, and lung disease
are owed compensation for their suffering, the Black community
deserves remuneration for slavery, segregation, redlining, police brutality, and the countless other discriminatory practices it has endured
for centuries.

Policymakers have a plethora of examples from which to draw for
such a reckoning. In 2016, Georgetown University publicly pledged
to extend preferential treatment to the descendants of the 272 slaves
it purchased in 1838. As the school's president, John DeGioia, noted,
"We cannot do our best work if we refuse to take ownership of such a
critical part of our history." Several universities followed suit, especially
after the massive worldwide Black Lives Matter marches in 2020.

Indeed, in 2020, the nation came as close as it has gotten in recent
years to having this long-overdue reckoning with its past. Members of
Congress were given the *New York Times*' "The 1619 Project" and hear-

ings were held in state and even federal chambers on the need to pay reparations. Some cities and municipalities, like Tulsa, Oklahoma, and the Bruce's Beach area in Los Angeles, unearthed long-buried records of racial terror and issued formal apologies. And as they did so, the forces of denial and forgetting grew to a fever pitch. As during every attempt at a racial reckoning—Reconstruction, the civil rights era—the force of the backlash was much greater than the force of progress. For to reckon with this history was to grieve so many cherished national myths. More importantly, to eliminate the nation's original sin was to denude racial hatred of its potency as a political weapon to divide the masses. To unite as a nation against those that divide us along the lines of race would mean accurately pointing our collective finger at the greed and corruption that have continued to thrive through distraction and scapegoating.

The bottom line is that racism, racist institutions, and racial inequity hurt *all* Americans. C. Vann Woodward noted the deterioration of the South's soul during the Jim Crow era. Frederick Douglass watched his white mistress change as she became a slave master. Her ownership of a human being warped and corrupted her previously decent character, turning her into a hateful person. James Baldwin worried about "the death of the heart" that racism had wrought on American culture, for "whoever debases others is debasing himself." Baldwin also understood that the "future of the Negro in this country is precisely as bright or as dark as the future of the country." The sooner Americans recognize that the fate of Black America is tied to the fate of white America, the faster it can achieve true democracy and shed the weight of historic injustices. Racism and its toxic practices have long afflicted the roots of American society; its political, economic, and social systems are sick with the rot, and, as a result, they all bear strange fruit. As long as the soil remains unturned and the systemic blight unaddressed, the harvest will be infected.

WHAT NEXT, THEN? AMERICANS must decide whether to keep embracing our history of racial tribalism or shed these divisions and go forward as one people, indivisible. Can the country's majoritarian democracy support a program intended solely to benefit the Black minority? It certainly did not in 1870, 1930, or 1960. However, there is reason to hope that this is more likely now than ever. We are facing another pivot point. The racial détente of the 1960s has fallen apart. The myth of post-racial America has been dispelled, and renewed tensions have erupted on the national stage as well as in segregated pockets of poverty in America.

ACKNOWLEDGMENTS

Thank you to Asia Meana for her brilliant editorial work, without which this book would not have been possible. Thank you to my Norton editor, Tom Mayer, whose kind, encouraging, and insightful comments created a warm and productive editorial process. Thank you to my agent, Amy Berkower, for the professionalism, care, and interest she brought to this book and every single other project. Thank you to Gavin McAlpin for your insightful and thorough editorial help. Thank you to my Race, Law, and Capitalism students at Harvard, Northwestern, and UCI Law schools, whose insightful comments and reflections in papers and in class have helped shaped the ideas in this book. Thank you to my daughters, Cyra, Lucia, and Ramona; my parents, Asad and Narima; and my siblings, Shima, Hediyeh, and Darius, for always believing in me and encouraging me and inspiring me with your own truth-seeking endeavors.

NOTES

INTRODUCTION

3   **"Segregation and poverty have created in the racial ghetto"**: National Advisory Commission on Civil Disorders, *The Kerner Report* (New York: Pantheon Books, 1988), 1.

9   **"a mass extinction event"**: Brad Miller, "The Foreclosure Crisis Was a Crime," *American Prospect*, August 13, 2019.

11   **"inherent savagery"**: *Johnson v. McIntosh*, 21 U.S. 543 (1823).

12   **As Christine Desan explains**: Christine Desan, *Making Money: Coin, Currency, and the Coming of Capitalism* (Oxford: Oxford University Press, 2014), 3–5.

CHAPTER 1: FROM CAPITAL TO CAPITALISTS

13   **The market value of slavery**: Jenny B. Wahl, "Slavery in the United States," Minnesota State University Moorhead.

14   **As one Presbyterian minister pontificated**: George D. Armstrong, *The Christian Doctrine of Slavery* (New York: C. Scribner, 1857), 134.

16   **promising forty acres of inexpensive land**: Walter L. Fleming, "Forty Acres and a Mule," *North American Review* 182, no. 594 (1906): 721–37.

18   **"a bargain between the North and South"**: James Baldwin, "A Talk to Teachers," in *The Price of the Ticket: Collected Nonfiction, 1948–1985* (Boston: Beacon, 1985), 334.

18   **relied on cotton from the American South**: Gene Dattel, *Cotton and Race in the Making of America: The Human Costs of Economic Power* (Lanham, MD: Ivan R. Dee, 2009), 5.

19   **"The empire of cotton is ensured"**: Sven Beckert, *Empire of Cotton* (New York: Knopf, 2014), 273, Kindle.

19 **The merchants and bankers from the old-world empire**: Edward E. Baptist, *The Half Has Never Been Told: Slavery and the Making of American Capitalism* (New York: Basic Books, 2014); Sven Beckert, *Empire of Cotton: A Global History* (New York: Penguin Books, 2014); and Dattel, *Cotton and Race in the Making of America.*

19 **compensation over hundreds of years**: Catherine Porter, Constant Méheut, Selam Gebrekidan, and Matt Apuzzo, "The Ransom: How a French Bank Captured Haiti," *New York Times*, May 20, 2022.

21 **"part banker, part despot"**: W.E.B. Du Bois, *Black Reconstruction in America, 1860–1880* (New York: Free Press, 1998), 386.

22 **"a system of peonage"**: Ibid., 390.

25 **As Du Bois put it**: W.E.B. Du Bois, *The Souls of Black Folk* (*Journal of Pan African Studies*, 2009), 37, e-book.

25 **One Missouri congressman**: E. Franklin Frazier, *Black Bourgeoisie: The Rise of a New Middle Class in the United States* (1957; repr., New York: Free Press Paperbacks, 1997), 143.

25 **Neither is fit to exercise**: Paul Lewinson, *Race, Class, and Party* (New York: Oxford University Press, 1932), 84–85.

25 **Philosopher Hannah Arendt**: Hannah Arendt, *The Origins of Totalitarianism* (New York: Harcourt, 1951), 159.

26 **Perhaps the most destructive**: *Plessy v. Ferguson*, 163 U.S. 537 (1896).

27 **"Southern trees"**: "Strange Fruit," by Billie Holiday and Abel Meeropol (1937).

27 **"the finest effort to achieve"**: Du Bois, *Black Reconstruction in America*, 634.

27 **"The slave went free"**: W.E.B. Du Bois, *Black Reconstruction in America* (London: Transaction, 2013), 26.

CHAPTER 2: THE EVOLUTION OF THE RACE PROBLEM

29 **In the words of contemporary Black thinker**: Ta-Nehisi Coates, *Between the World and Me* (New York: Spiegel & Grau, 2015).

30 **"If we had a bank of our own"**: W. P. Burrell and Thomas W. Mitchell, *Twenty-Five Years History of the Grand Fountain of the United Order of True Reformers, 1881–1905* (Richmond, VA: Grand Fountain, 1909), 45–47.

30 **"The great all absorbing interest"**: Maggie L. Walker, *A Testimonial of Love Tendered Mrs. Maggie L. Walker: 25 Years of Service* (Richmond, VA: St. Luke Press, 1925), 56.

30 **It was said of Walker that**: Ibid.

30 **These institutions were mired**: James Baldwin, "The Harlem Ghetto," in

Baldwin: Collected Essays, ed. Toni Morrison (New York: Library of America, 1998), 43.

31   **Addressing a largely white audience**: Booker T. Washington, "Atlanta Compromise Speech," in *The Booker T. Washington Papers*, vol. 3, ed. Louis R. Harlan (Urbana: University of Illinois Press, 1974), 583–87.

31   **"the Southern white man has needed his labor"**: Thomas Dixon Jr., "Booker T. Washington and the Negro," *Saturday Evening Post*, August 19, 1905. Washington, Dixon noted, was not "training Negroes to take their place in any industrial system of the South in which the white man can direct or control him."

32   **Du Bois was staunchly supportive**: W.E.B. Du Bois, *The Negro in Business* (Atlanta, GA: Atlanta University Press, 1899), 5.

32   **it was a sure way to cement**: Ibid.

32   **no real chance of a thriving Black economy**: Ibid.

32   **"house servants became barbers"**: John Seder and Berkeley G. Burrell, *Getting It Together: Black Businessmen in America* (New York: Harcourt Brace Jovanovich, 1971), 10.

33   **The historian Clifford Kuhn**: Clifford M. Kuhn, Harlon E. Joye, and E. Bernard West, *Living in Atlanta: An Oral History of the City, 1914–1948* (Athens: University of Georgia Press, 2005), 106.

34   **this dynamic was not often possible**: M. S. Stuart, *An Economic Detour: A History of Insurance in the Lives of American Negroes* (McGrath, 1969), 36. Cited in John Sibley Butler, *Entrepreneurship and Self-Help Among Black Americans* (Albany: State University of New York Press, 2005), 118–19.

35   **Insidious racist notions**: Frederick L. Hoffman, *Race Traits and Tendencies of the American Negro* (New York: Macmillan, 1896), 95; and Robert William Fogel and Stanley L. Engerman, *Time on the Cross: The Economics of American Negro Slavery* (New York: W. W. Norton, 1995), 125.

35   **"Go to Durham and see"**: Walter B. Weare, *Black Business in the New South: A Social History of the North Carolina Mutual Life Insurance Company* (Chicago: University of Illinois Press, 1973), 4–5.

35   **As the mayor of Durham**: Butler, *Entrepreneurship and Self-Help*, 193, referring to an article in the *Durham Morning Herald*, September 16, 1927; quoted in Thomas H. Houck, *A Newspaper History of Race Relations in Durham, North Carolina, 1900–1940* (Durham, NC: Duke University Press, 1941), 81.

36   **"Even housewives refused"**: "Blood and Oil," *The Survey* 46 (June 11, 1921): 369.

37   **They poured into Greenwood**: W.E.B. Du Bois, "The Massacre of East St. Louis," *The Crisis* 14, no. 4 (August 2017), 158–59.

37   **"Among them were"**: John Sibley Butler, *Entrepreneurship and Self-Help* (New York: State University of New York Press, 1991), 229.

39   **"The Democratic idea"**: "Bryan's 'Cross of Gold' Speech: Mesmerizing the Masses," History Matters: The U.S. Survey Course on the Web.

40   **"We demand a national currency"**: Gerhard Peters and John T. Woolley, "Populist Party Platform of 1892," American Presidency Project.

41   **Or as "hard money" proponent**: Arun Kundnani, "Disembowel Enoch Powell," *Dissent*, April 18, 2018.

41   **Proponents of gold-backed currency**: Michael O'Malley, *Face Value: The Entwined Histories of Money and Race in America* (Chicago: University of Chicago Press, 2022), 134.

42   **Wilson sought to build**: Jacob S. Hacker and Paul Pierson, *American Amnesia: How the War on Government Led Us to Forget What Made America Prosper* (New York: Simon & Schuster, 2016), 104–05.

42   **"Our system of credit is privately concentrated"**: Woodrow Wilson, "Address to Congress on the Banking System," June 23, 1913, in *The Papers of Woodrow Wilson*, ed. Arthur S. Link, vol. 28 (Princeton, NJ: Princeton University Press, 1978), 293–95.

43   **"subhuman or a beast"**: Khalil Gibran Muhammad, *The Condemnation of Blackness: Race, Crime, and the Making of Modern Urban America* (Cambridge, MA: Harvard University Press, 2010), 85–86.

44   **"as destitute of morals"**: Ibid.

44   **"negro is monkey-like"**: Ibid.

44   **He called this perversion of science**: W.E.B. Du Bois, "Evolution of the Race Problem," in *Proceedings of the National Negro Conference* (New York: N.p., 1909), 142–58.

45   **"For white Americans of every ideological stripe"**: Muhammad, *Condemnation of Blackness*, 4.

CHAPTER 3: THE CATCH-22 OF BLACK BANKS

47   **In his poem**: Langston Hughes, "The South," *The Collected Poems of Langston Hughes*, ed. Arnold Rampersad (New York: Vintage Books, 1995), 26–27.

48   "cities of destruction": E. Franklin Frazier, *The Negro Family in the United States* (Chicago: University of Chicago Press, 1939), 386–87.

48   For while the Black community: James Baldwin, *The Evidence of Things Not Seen* (New York: Henry Holt, 1985), 25.

49   "If they can make the leaders move": William Lorenz Katz, ed., *The American Negro: His History and Literature* (New York: Arno Press and the New York Times, 1968), 131; and Chicago Commission on Race Relations, *The Negro in Chicago: A Study of Race Relations and a Race Riot* (Chicago: University of Chicago Press, 1922), 131.

49   Despite the fact that Binga: John A. Carroll, "The Great American Bubble," *Real America Magazine*, April 1935, 16–20.

50   "unless the applicant can show": John H. Bracey Jr., "The Negro Banker in the United States: A Study in American Economic Development" (PhD diss., University of Chicago, 1938), 45.

51   One white teller of the Chelsea Exchange Bank: Earl Louis Brown, "Negro Banks in the United States" (MA thesis, Boston University, 1930), 28.

51   As George Bernard Shaw put it: George Bernard Shaw, *Man and Superman* (London, 1903), quoted in Robert Lee Grant, *The Star-Spangled Hustle* (New York: Lippincott, 1972), 76.

51   His pro-segregation rhetoric: David Van Leeuwen, "Marcus Garvey and the Universal Negro Improvement Association," accessed January 29, 2017, http://nationalhumanitiescenter.org/tserve/twenty/tkeyinfo/garvey.htm.

51   "the most dangerous enemy of the Negro race": W.E.B. Du Bois, "Marcus Garvey," *The Crisis* 28, no. 6 (October 1924): 266.

51   He was an advocate for capitalism: Marcus Garvey, *Life and Lessons* (Berkeley: University of California Press, 1987), xxvii.

52   Richard R. Wright Sr.: Richard R. Wright Jr., "The Financial Condition of Our People" (address delivered before the Philadelphia Preachers' Meeting), *Christian Recorder*, May 19, 1921.

53   Even Maggie Walker: Shennette Garrett-Scott, *Banking on Freedom: Black Women in U.S. Finance Before the New Deal* (New York: Columbia University Press, 2019), 152.

56   "They thus live from day to day": Gunnar Myrdal, *An American Dilemma: The Negro Problem and Modern Democracy* (New York: Harper & Brothers, 1944), 205.

57   Against these conditions: W.E.B. Du Bois, "A Negro Nation Within the Nation," *Current History (1916–1940)* 42, no. 3 (1935): 265–70.

57   In *The Mis-education of the Negro*: Carter G. Woodson, *The Mis-education of the Negro* (New York: Penguin Classics, 2023), 33.

57   "skillful exploitation of the Negro masses": Abram L. Harris, *The Negro as Capitalist* (Whitefish, MT: Kessinger, 2010), 175.

59   The system was so intricately rigged: W.E.B. Du Bois, *The Souls of Black Folk* (*Journal of Pan African Studies*, 2009), 128, e-book.

CHAPTER 4: THE NEW DEAL FOR WHITE AMERICA

60   Housing starts were: Melvin L. Oliver and Thomas M. Shapiro, *Black Wealth, White Wealth: A New Perspective on Racial Inequality* (New York: Routledge, 2006), 17; and Kenneth T. Jackson, *Crabgrass Frontier: The Suburbanization of the United States* (New York: Oxford University Press, 1987), 205.

61   The FHA also produced protocol: John R. Walter, "The 3-6-3 Rule: An Urban Myth?," *Federal Reserve Bank of Richmond Economic Quarterly* 92, no. 1 (Winter 2006): 51.

61   These GSEs fostered a secondary market: Louis Hyman, *Debtor Nation: The History of America in Red Ink* (Princeton, NJ: Princeton University Press, 2011), 55.

61   The government created the platform: The federal guarantee revolutionized mortgages because the fund insured 90 percent of individual home mortgages. According to Julian Zimmerman, FHA commissioner in the 1950s, when the scheme was first proposed, "it was such an innovation that many considered it radical and unworkable." He later remarked, "It was the last hope of private enterprise. The alternative was socialization of the housing industry." FHA, *FHA Story in Summary, 1934–1959* (Washington, DC: GPO, 1959), 4; cited in Hyman, *Debtor Nation*, 53.

62   For example, between 1934 and 1980: Credit Union National Association, "Credit Union Trends Report: Long-Run Trends (1939–Present)," accessed May 29, 2025, https://news.cuna.org/ext/resources/CUMag_Misc/issues/CUMag_2018-03.pdf.

62   Total commercial bank branches: National Credit Union Administration, *Annual Report 1980*, 3, https://ncua.gov/files/annual-reports/AR1980.pdf; and Federal Deposit Insurance Corporation, "BankFind Suite: Find Annual Historical Bank Data," accessed May 29, 2025, https://banks.data.fdic.gov/explore/historical/.

62   Some 11,000 S&Ls: Mehrsa Baradaran, *How the Other Half Banks* (Cambridge, MA: Harvard University Press, 2015), chapter 3.

62   **"future of *essential democracy*"**: Franklin D. Roosevelt, "Inaugural Address of the President," March 4, 1933, National Archives, https://www.archives .gov/education/lessons/fdr-inaugural, accessed May 5, 2025 (italics mine).

64   **"You cannot put the Negro and the white man"**: Ira Katznelson, *When Affirmative Action Was White* (New York: W. W. Norton, 2005), 60.

64   **Slowly but effectively, the New Deal**: Katznelson, *When Affirmative Action Was White*, 48.

67   **The FHA's *Underwriting Manual***: Dalton Conley, *Being Black, Living in the Red: Race, Wealth, and Social Policy in America* (Berkeley: University of California Press, 1999), 37.

67   **The manual stated**: Melvin L. Oliver and Thomas M. Shapiro, *Black Wealth/White Wealth* (New York: Routledge, 1997), 18; Jackson, *Crabgrass*, 208; and Federal Housing Authority, *Underwriting Manual* (Washington, DC, 1936), part 2, paragraph 233.

70   **Chicago native Dempsey J. Travis**: Dempsey Travis, *An Autobiography of Black Chicago* (Evanston, IL: Agate Bolden, 2014), 128–29.

70   **"The cost of maintaining black pride"**: Ibid., 163.

71   **He saw the "flagrant ignorance" and racism**: Douglas Martin, "M. Moran Weston, 91, Priest and Banker of Harlem, Dies," *New York Times*, May 22, 2002; Charlayne Hunter, "Church in Harlem Plays Vital Role in Community," *New York Times*, December 6, 1970; and James Barron, "When Churches Go into the Business of Housing," *New York Times*, May 13, 1979.

71   **King drafted the ambitious blueprint**: Martin Luther King, "We Are Still Walking," *Liberation*, December 1956, https://kinginstitute.stanford.edu/ king-papers/documents/we-are-still-walking.

72   **Frazier referred to Washington's promised land**: E. Franklin Frazier, *Black Bourgeoisie: The Rise of a New Middle Class in the United States* (1957; repr., New York: Free Press Paperbacks, 1997), 25, 109.

73   **What was formerly the Bank of Italy**: "Bank of America: The Humble Beginnings of a Large Bank," Office of the Comptroller of the Currency, http://www.occ.gov/about/what-we-do/history/giannini-bank-article -html-version.html.

74   **The first act of mass civil disobedience**: National Archives, Executive Order 8802: Prohibition of Discrimination in the Defense Industry, June 25, 1941.

74   **Fueled by the observation that white businesses**: Abram L. Harris, *The Negro as Capitalist* (Whitefish, MT: Kessinger Publishing, 2010), 177.

75 **The Harlem Labor Union took up this cause**: Albon Holsey, speech to the National Association of Teachers in Colored Schools, Jackson, MS, July 1929.

75 **"The time has arrived in America"**: Hubert H. Humphrey, "1948 Democratic National Convention Address," July 14, 1948, Philadelphia.

76 **"on the white male heterosexual breadwinning wage"**: Jonathan Levy, *Ages of American Capitalism* (New York: Random House, 2021), 551.

CHAPTER 5: CIVIL RIGHTS DREAMS, ECONOMIC NIGHTMARES

77 **A part of the written speech**: Martin Luther King Jr., "Address to the New York State Civil War Centennial Commission," New York, September 12, 1962.

78 **"complete the work begun by Abraham Lincoln"**: John F. Kennedy, "Remarks Recorded for Emancipation Proclamation Centennial Ceremony," Lincoln Memorial, Washington, DC, September 22, 1962.

78 **"There is little value in a Negro obtaining"**: John F. Kennedy, Special Message to the Congress on Civil Rights and Job Opportunities," June 19, 1963, American Presidency Project.

78 **The Senate, a body that acted**: Robert Caro, *Master of the Senate: The Years of Lyndon Johnson* (New York: Random House, 2002), 65.

79 **If, as Bayard Rustin noted**: Bayard Rustin, "Funding Full Citizenship," *Council Journal* 6, no. 3 (December 1967).

79 **During a similar incident**: David J. Garrow, *Bearing the Cross: Martin Luther King, Jr., and the Southern Christian Leadership Conference* (1986; repr., New York: Perennial Classics, 2004), 439.

80 **As a grocery store in Chicago**: Sauter Van Gordon, "Flames Erase Long Stretch of Chicago's Madison Street," *Washington Post*, April 7, 1968, A7.

80 **The first draft of the report**: National Advisory Commission on Civil Disorders, *The Kerner Report* (New York: Pantheon Books, 1988), 1.

80 **The commission resolutely endorsed**: Ibid., 141.

81 **An "urban sharecropping system"**: David Caplovitz, *The Poor Pay More: Consumer Practices of Low-Income Families* (New York: Free Press, 1963), 25, 100.

81 **As the debt historian Louis Hyman**: Louis Hyman, *Debtor Nation: The History of America in Red Ink* (Princeton, NJ: Princeton University Press, 2011), 193.

82 **He and his team**: Federal Trade Commission Report on Credit Practices, *Consumer Credit and the Poor* (Washington, DC: U.S. Government Printing

Office, 1968), 80–85; *Financial Institutions and the Urban Crisis: Hearings Before the Subcommittee on Financial Institutions of the Committee on Banking and Currency*, U.S. Senate, 90th Cong., 2nd Sess. on private investment in the inner city (September 30 and October 1– 4, 1968) (Washington, DC: U.S. Government Printing Office, 1968), 151, 324–27; and Proxmire, *U.S. Senator Proxmire Reports to You From Washington*, 1964–77.

82   **He believed that "no conceivable increase"**: Ibid., 9, 13.

82   **The Small Business Administration (SBA)**: Ibid., 94–95.

83   **Proxmire, who believed strongly in credit unions**: Proxmire, *U.S. Senator Proxmire Reports to You From Washington*, 1964–77.

83   **The survey found that 85 percent of ghetto consumers**: Caplovitz, *The Poor Pay More*, 95.

84   **Though the Lyndon B. Johnson administration**: House Committee, Economic Opportunity Act of 1964, 305.

84   **He attested that**: Lyndon B. Johnson, "Commencement Address at Howard University," June 4, 1965.

84   **Here, he was directly quoting King**: Martin Luther King Jr., *Why We Can't Wait* (New York: Signet Books, 1964), 134.

85   **Moynihan pointed directly at high rates**: Daniel P. Moynihan, *The Negro Family: The Case for National Action* (Washington, DC: Office of Policy Planning and Research, 1965).

86   **"daily violence"**: Martin Luther King Jr., *The Autobiography of Martin Luther King, Jr.*, ed. Clayborne Carson (New York: Warner Books, 1998), 340.

86   **A poll taken in 1966**: William Brink and Louis Harris, *Black and White: A Study of U.S. Racial Attitudes Today* (New York: Simon & Schuster, 1967), 100, 120.

86   **"silent (white) majority"**: Malcolm X, *Malcolm X Speaks: Selected Speeches and Statements*, ed. George Breitman (New York: Grove, 1965), 23–44.

87   **Ronald Reagan's campaign for governor**: Gerard DeGroot, *Selling Ronald Reagan: The Emergency of a President* (London: I.B. Tauris, 2015), 162.

88   **King, who drew influence from Mahatma Gandhi's**: King, *Autobiography of Martin Luther King, Jr.*, 70.

88   **"I've seen my dream shattered"**: Clayborne Carson and Peter Holloran, eds., *A Knock at Midnight: Inspiration from the Great Sermons of Reverend Martin Luther King, Jr.* (New York: IPM/Warner Books, 1998), 61.

89   **Gerald McKnight writes that**: Gerald McKnight, *The Last Crusade: Martin Luther King, Jr., the FBI, and the Poor People's Campaign* (Boulder, CO:

Westview, 1998), 20–22; and King, *Autobiography of Martin Luther King, Jr.*, 353.

90   **He and the other new Black leaders**: Peniel E. Joseph, *Stokely: A Life* (New York: Basic Civitas Books, 2014), 104.

90   **"One needed a handle"**: James Baldwin, *The Fire Next Time* (New York: Vintage International), 21.

90   **"Our people have to be made to see"**: Malcolm X, *Malcolm X Speaks: Selected Speeches and Statements*, ed. George Breitman (New York: Grove, 1965), 39.

91   **"Whenever any form of government becomes destructive"**: Joshua Bloom and Waldo E. Martin Jr., *Black Against Empire: The History and Politics of the Black Panther Party* (Oakland: University of California Press, 2016), 70–72.

93   **There were more than twenty civil rights**: For examples, see Community Reinvestment Act 12 U.S.C. § 2901 (1977) (stating that regulated banking institutions must show they are meeting the credit need within the communities where they do business, including for low- to moderate-income community members); Fair Housing Act, 42 U.S.C. § 3604 (1968) (making it unlawful to discriminate when extending housing credit on the basis of "race, color, religion, sex, familial status, or national origin"); Federal Trade Commission Improvement Act, 15 U.S.C. § 57a (1980) (gives the Federal Reserve the power to identify unfair practices, including discrimination, and to construct regulations to prohibit and enforce against these unfair acts); Home Mortgage Disclosure Act, 12 U.S.C. § 2803 (1975) (requiring that depository institutions report the race, ethnicity, sex, and income of borrowers and applicants and the prices on these loans to ensure that discriminatory practices are not being pursued); and Women's Business Ownership Act, 15 U.S.C. § 631 (1988) (affords women who own businesses protection against discrimination based on gender, such as requiring a legitimate justification for denying credit). See also David A. Skeel Jr., *Racial Dimensions of Credit and Bankruptcy*, *Washington and Lee Law Review* 61, no. 4 (2004): 1695, 1706–12.

93   **The largest and most important**: 42 U.S.C. §§ 3601–19 (1968); 15 U.S.C.A. § 1691 (1974); 12 U.S.C.A. § 2801–10 (1975); and 12 U.S.C.A. § 2901–09 (1977).

93   **"Credit allocation schemes"**: Greta R. Krippner, *Capitalizing on Crisis* (Cambridge, MA: Harvard University Press, 2011), 70, Kindle.

94   **Their campaign came to be labeled**: The Humphrey-Hawkins bill, which

eventually passed in 1978, mandated that the Federal Reserve focus on a dual mandate of securing full employment as well as controlling inflation. Helen Lachs Ginsburg, "Historical Amnesia: The Humphrey-Hawkins Act, Full Employment and Employment as a Right," *Review of Black Political Economy* 39, no. 1 (2012).

94   **The final bill, which passed in 1978**: Ginsburg, "Historical Amnesia."

94   **"That was the problem—money"**: John David Skrentny, *The Ironies of Affirmative Action: Politics, Culture, and Justice in America* (Chicago: University of Chicago Press, 1996), 99.

95   **"The cost of one modern heavy bomber"**: Dwight D. Eisenhower, "The Chance for Peace," address delivered before the American Society of Newspaper Editors, April 16, 1953, American Presidency Project.

95   **"to rebuild our whole planet"**: King, Address to the New York State Civil War Centennial Commission.

96   **"I knew that America would never invest"**: Martin Luther King Jr., "Beyond Vietnam," speech at Riverside Church Meeting, New York, NY, April 4, 1967; in Clayborne Carson et al., eds., *The Eyes on the Prize: A Reader and Guide* (New York: Penguin, 1987), 201–04.

CHAPTER 6: THE DECOY OF BLACK CAPITALISM

97   **Alan Greenspan, a Nixon campaign adviser**: Sebastian Mallaby, *The Man Who Knew: The Life and Times of Alan Greenspan* (New York: Penguin Press, 2016).

98   **If Black issues mattered at all**: Ibid., 121.

98   **As Robinson summarized it**: J. Christopher Schutz, *Jackie Robinson: An Integrated Life* (Lanham, MD: Rowman & Littlefield, 2016).

99   **What created the anger**: Mallaby, *The Man Who Knew*, 107–08.

100   **"Instead of government jobs"**: Dean J. Kotlowski, *Nixon's Civil Rights* (Cambridge, MA: Harvard University Press, 2001), 106.

100   **Black leaders had certainly been calling**: interview with Roy Innis, *U.S. News & World Report*, November 25, 1968, 60.

101   **The next item on Romney's agenda**: Kotlowski, *Nixon's Civil Rights*, 55; and "Balanced Communities" and "Position Paper on Open Communities (II)," n.d., Box 10, Richard C. Van Duesen Subject Files, Record Group 207, General Records of the Department of Housing and Urban Development, National Archives, College Park, MD.

102   **"convinced that while legal segregation"**: Nikole Hannah-Jones, "Living Apart," ProPublica, June 25, 2015.

102 **In the words of Dempsey Travis:** Dempsey Travis, *An Autobiography of Black Chicago* (Evanston, IL: Agate Bolden, 2014), 156.

102 **"Integration is dead as a doornail":** "Roy Innis Asserts Integration Is 'Dead,'" *New York Times*, April 24, 1977, 44.

103 **"Integration today means the man":** "What We Want," *New York Review of Books* 7 (September 22, 1966): 5–6, 8.

103 **It was an outright call for reparations:** James Foreman, "Total Control as the Only Solution for the Economic Needs of Black People," speech presented at the National Black Economic Development Conference, Detroit, MI, April 26,1969, 7.

104 **"For the past five years":** campaign ad, Nixon, "The Wrong Road," starts at 1:13, "Presidential Campaign Commercials," https://www.c-span.org/video/?153104-1/presidential-campaign-commercials-1968.

104 **He insisted that the government's:** Draft speech, Human Dignity, First Draft, 4/6/68, labeled RN's Copy, File 8, ARRA 24, Nixon Library (on file with author).

104 **They want the pride:** Richard Nixon, "Address Accepting the Presidential Nomination at the Republican National Convention in Miami Beach, Florida," August 8, 1968, American Presidency Project.

105 **Even the *New York Times*:** Tom Wicker, "In the Nation: A Coalition for What?," *New York Times*, May 19, 1968.

106 **Of course, demand for Black businesses:** Theodore L. Cross, "A White Paper on Black Capitalism," in *Black Economic Development*, ed. William Haddad and G. Douglas Pugh (Englewood Cliffs, NJ: Prentice-Hall, 1969), 25–26.

106 **Stans reiterated that the program:** Arthur I. Blaustein and Geoffrey Faux, *The Star-Spangled Hustle* (Anchor, 1973), 155–57.

108 **"two dozen summer jobs":** Whitney M. Young Jr., "It's Good Business for Business to Solve Social Problems," *New York Times*, January 11, 1970.

108 **unmotivated by the weak incentives:** Michael Brower and Doyle Little, "White Help for Black Business," *Harvard Business Review*, 48 (1970).

109 **As John Ehrlichman wrote:** Hugh Davis Graham, "Richard Nixon and Civil Rights," *Presidential Studies Quarterly* 26, no. 1 (1996), citing John D. Ehrlichman, *Witness to Power* (New York: Simon & Schuster, 1982).

111 **"It cannot be found in a backwater":** Andrew Brimmer, "The Trouble with Black Capitalism," *Nation's Business*, May 1969, 79.

111 **"It just happens":** William L. Henderson and Larry C. Ledebur, "Programs for the Economic Development of the American Negro Commu-

nity: The Moderate Approach," *American Journal of Economics and Sociology* 30, no. 1 (1971), and Robert L. Allen, *Black Awakening in Capitalist America: An Analytic History* (Garden City, NY: Doubleday, 1969), 200.

112   **"The critical question is, of course"**: Letter from Alan Greenspan to candidate Nixon, Nixon Presidential Library files, Subject: "The Urban Riots of the 1960's," September 26, 1967.

CHAPTER 7: THE FREE MARKET CONFRONTS BLACK POVERTY

116   **"Measured by any benchmark"**: *Bakke v. University of California*, 438 U.S. 265, 395–96 (1978).

116   **Writing for a conservative majority**: *City of Richmond v. J. A. Croson Co.*, 488 U.S. 469, 505–06 (1989).

117   **"As a democratic people"**: Ronald Reagan, "Remarks on Signing the Bill Making the Birthday of Martin Luther King, Jr., a National Holiday," November 2, 1983, Ronald Reagan Presidential Library & Museum.

118   **He linked his belief in market deregulation**: Republican National Convention, "Republican Party Platform of 1988: An American Vision: For Our Children and Our Future," August 16, 1988, American Presidency Project.

118   **"afford socially and economically disadvantaged"**: Ibid.

118   **In place of tangible solutions**: Ibid.

118   **"draw a green line of prosperity"**: Committee on Resolutions, Republican National Convention, "Republican Party Platform of 1984," August 20, 1984, American Presidency Project.

118   **"increase, strengthen, and reinvigorate"**: Republican National Convention, "Republican Party Platform of 1988."

119   **In a 1982 speech**: "Minority Enterprise Development Week," in *Encyclopedia of African American Business*, ed. Jessie Carney Smith (Westport, CT: Greenwood, 2006), 2:536.

119   **All of this was cribbed**: Heritage Foundation, *Mandate for Leadership: Policy Management in a Conservative Administration* (Washington, DC: Heritage Foundation, 1980)—see especially the chapters on the Justice Department and civil rights); Nancy MacLean, *Democracy in Chains: The Deep History of the Radical Right's Stealth Plan for America* (New York: Viking, 2017), chapter 9; and Thomas Byrne Edsall and Mary D. Edsall, *Chain Reaction: The Impact of Race, Rights, and Taxes on American Politics* (New York: W. W. Norton, 1992), 55–70.

119   **both President Carter and President Reagan passed initiatives**: Jimmy

Carter, "Executive Order 12138: Women's Business Enterprise," May 18, 1979, American Presidency Project; and Ronald Reagan, "Annual Report to the Congress on the State of Small Business," March 19, 1984, in Ronald Reagan Presidential Library & Museum.

119 **President Reagan's Women's Business Ownership Act**: Women's Business Ownership Act of 1988, Public Law No. 100-533 (1988) (current version at 41 U.S.C. § 1713).

120 **"You want to know"**: Dan Baum, "Legalize it All," *Harper's Magazine,* April 2016.

121 **Poverty, segregation, and heavy policing**: Adam Walinsky, "Crack as Scapegoat," *New York Times,* September 16, 1986.

122 **"I did not fight for the right of black people"**: "Excerpts from Clinton's Speech to Black Ministers," *New York Times,* November 14, 1993.

122 **eight hundred thousand Black men**: Justice Policy Institute, *Cellblocks or Classrooms? The Funding of Higher Education and Corrections and Its Impact on African American Men* (Washington, DC, 2002).

122 **Clinton slashed welfare**: Kathryn J. Edin and H. Luke Shaefer, *$2.00 a Day: Living on Almost Nothing in America* (Boston: Mariner Books, 2015), 17.

123 **Clinton's urban poverty programs**: Background on The Clinton-Gore Administration's Community Development Record, November 4, 1999, https://clintonwhitehouse3.archives.gov/WH/New/New_Markets_Nov/factsheets/comdevl.html (noting that the initiatives included Empowerment Zones, Enterprise Communities, expansions of the Low-Income Housing Tax Credit, and the Community Development Financial Institutions Fund).

123 **His Department of Housing and Urban Development**: Julia S. Rubin and Gregory M. Stankiewicz, "Evaluating the Impact of Federal Community Economic Development Policies on Targeted Populations: The Case of the New Markets Initiatives of 2000," *Proceedings: Federal Reserve Bank of Chicago* (February 2003).

123 **"The cornerstone of such a model"**: Michael E. Porter, *The Competitive Advantage of the Inner City, Harvard Business Review* 73, no. 3 (May–June 1995): 55–71.

124 **Because the Supreme Court**: *City of Richmond v. J. A. Croson Co.*, 488 U.S. 469, 505–06 (1989). In this case, the Supreme Court agreed to end the contract set-aside program. The court rejected Richmond's claim that "past societal discrimination" could justify a racial preference.

124 **The final conference report**: *Community Capitalism: Rediscovering the Mar-*

kets of America's Urban Neighborhoods, Ninety-First American Assembly, Columbia University, April 17–20, 1997 (New York: American Assembly, 1997), 3.

124   **Vice President Al Gore endorsed**: American Assembly, *Community Capitalism: Rediscovering the Markets of America's Urban Neighborhoods* (New York: Columbia University, 1997). According to Clinton official Gene Sperling, the legislation was meant to create "incentives that would encourage the private sector to find profits and create opportunities." Mehrsa Baradaran, *How the Other Half Banks* (Cambridge, MA: Harvard University Press, 2015).

124   **Clinton's "community capitalism" program**: Riegle Community Development and Regulatory Improvement Act of 1994, Public Law No. 103-325, 108 Stat. 2160 (codified as amended in scattered sections of 12 U.S.C.).

124   **The bank's ambitious mission**: Katharine Esty, "Lessons from Muhammad Yunus and the Grameen Bank: Leading Long-term Organizational Change Successfully," *OD Practitioner* 43, no. 1 (2011).

125   **"You have to go into these areas"**: Jann S. Wenner, Hunter S. Thompson, William Greider, and P. J. O Rourke, "Bill Clinton: The Rolling Stone Interview," *Rolling Stone*, September 17, 1992.

127   **The crisis eradicated 53 percent**: Zoë Carpenter, "Five Years After Dodd-Frank, 'It's Still a Financial System That Needs Reform,'" *The Nation*, July 23, 2015.

127   **"extinction event" that**: Brad Miller, "The Foreclosure Crisis Was a Crime," *American Prospect*, August 13, 2019.

127   **"How many of you people"**: Rick Santelli, remarks on CNBC's *Squawk Box*, February 19, 2009, archived by CNBC, https://www.cnbc.com/video/2009/02/19/cnbc-original-video-rick-santelli-rant.html.

128   **While Wall Street received**: Nick Carey, "Regulators Close Well-Connected ShoreBank," Reuters, August 20, 2010.

128   **Glenn Beck used**: "ShoreBank's Tangled Web," *The Glenn Beck Program*, Fox News, May 21, 2010.

128   **The bank's assets were taken**: AP, "ShoreBank Fails; Will Be Reincarnated as Urban Partnership Bank," *Crain's Detroit Business*, August 22, 2010.

129   **But commission member**: David Min, "Faulty Conclusions Built on Shoddy Foundations," SSRN, February 2011.

129   **Wallison's claim**: Charles W. Calomiris and Stephen H. Haber, *Fragile by Design* (Princeton, NJ: Princeton University Press, 2014); and Eliza-

beth Laderman and Carolina Reid, "CRA Lending During the Subprime Meltdown," *Revisiting the CRA: Perspectives on the Future of the Community Reinvestment Act* (Federal Reserve Banks of Boston and San Francisco, February 2009), 115.

130   **Yet, also like affirmative action**: "Civil Rights Chief Faults CRA as Toothless Legislation," *American Banker*, May 21, 1992.

130   **Republican members of the House blamed**: Kenneth J. Cooper, "Loans to Minorities Did Not Cause Housing Crisis, Study Finds," *New America Media*, February 9, 2011.

130   **A Fox News commentator remarked**: Monica Crowley on *Your World with Neil Cavuto*, Fox News, October 10, 2011, as reported by Remington Shepard, "Still Wrong: Crowley Revives Myth That Community Reinvestment Act Caused Financial Crisis," Media Matters for America, October 11, 2011.

130   **This sort of resentment**: Christopher S. Parker and Matt A. Barreto, *Change They Can't Believe In: The Tea Party and Reactionary Politics in America* (Princeton, NJ: Princeton University Press, 2014), 1–3.

131   **The theory that the CRA**: Timothy Geithner, *Stress Test: Reflections on a Financial Crisis* (New York: Crown, 2014), 391–92. See also Senator Robert Menendez, "Fed Chairman Bernanke Confirms to Menendez That Community Reinvestment Act Is Not to Blame for Foreclosure Crisis," press release, December 2, 2008; David Min, "Why Wallison Is Wrong About the Genesis of the U.S. Housing Crisis," Center for American Progress, July 12, 2011; and Ben S. Bernanke, *The Courage to Act* (New York: W. W. Norton, 2015).

131   **The majority of the crisis-causing**: Neil Bhutta and Glenn B. Canner, "Did the CRA Cause the Mortgage Meltdown?," *Community Dividend*, March 1, 2009. See also Governor Randall S. Kroszner, "Speech at the Confronting Concentrated Poverty Forum," Federal Reserve, December 3, 2008.

132   **As the Center for Responsible Lending**: Tami Luhby, "Housing Crisis Hits Blacks Hardest," CNN, October 19, 2010.

132   **Republican Senator Phil Gramm**: Financial Services Modernization Act of 1999, 145 Cong. Rec. S4736 (May 5, 1999).

132   **"It's unbelievable"**: Jeffrey Marshall, "Lenders Cry Foul over Fair Lending Prosecutions," *American Banker*, October 1, 1994.

133   **They reason that the minority applicants**: See generally Richard Sander and Stuart Taylor Jr., *Mismatch: How Affirmative Action Hurts Students It's*

Intended to Help, and Why Universities Won't Admit It (New York: Basic Books, 2012).

134   **One massive Federal Reserve study**: Board of Governors of the Federal Reserve System, "Home Mortgage Disclosure Act: Expanded Data on Residential Lending," *Federal Reserve Bulletin* (November 1991): 859–81.

134   **"homeowners in high-income"**: HUD, "Unequal Burden: Income and Racial Disparities in Subprime Lending," https://archives.hud.gov/reports/subprime/subprime.cfm.

134   **"This is a system of segregation"**: Rob Wells, "Bank Mired in Loan Bias Scandal," *Register-Guard* (Eugene, OR), December 27, 1992, D1.

EPILOGUE: TOWARD FUNDAMENTAL REFORM

139   **In 1948, W.E.B. Du Bois**: W.E.B. Du Bois, *The Souls of Black Folk* (*Journal of Pan African Studies*, 2009), 257, e-book.

139   **On average, a Black customer will pay**: Cass Sunstein and Richard Thayer, *Nudge* (New Haven, CT: Yale University Press, 2008), 134.

140   **Indeed, Black people are twice**: "Payday Lending in America: Who Borrows, Where They Borrow, and Why," Pew Charitable Trusts, July 2012.

140   **Most of the other lawsuits**: Paul Kiel and Annie Waldman, "The Color of Debt: How Collection Suits Squeeze Black Neighborhoods," ProPublica, October 8, 2015; see also Breno Braga et al., "Local Conditions and Debt in Collections" (working paper, Urban Institute, 2016).

140   **Impoverished Black Americans**: Kiel and Waldman, "The Color of Debt."

143   **Most people buy a cup of coffee**: U.S. Department of the Treasury, "Freedman's Bank Forum," September 23, 2016, video, accessed May 29, 2025, https://home.treasury.gov/news/webcasts/2016 (the pertinent dialogue starts at 19:00).

143   **Data show that when controlling**: Darrick Hamilton, William A. Darity Jr., Anne E. Price, Vishnu Sridharan, and Rebecca Tippett, *Umbrellas Don't Make It Rain: Why Studying and Working Hard Isn't Enough for Black Americans* (New York: New School, Duke Center for Social Equity, and Insight, 2015); see also Darrick Hamilton and William A. Darity Jr., "The Political Economy of Education, Financial Literacy, and the Racial Wealth Gap," *Federal Reserve Bank of St. Louis Review* 99, no. 1 (2017), https://socialequity.duke.edu/wp-content/uploads/2019/10/The-Political-Economy-of-Education-Financial-Literacy-and-the-Racial-Wealth-Gap.pdf; and Maury Gittleman and Edward N. Wolff, "Racial Differences in

Patterns of Wealth Accumulation," *Journal of Human Resources* 39, no. 1 (Winter 2004): 193–227.

143   **the white middle class fares**: Andre Perry, Jonathan Rothwell, and David Harshbarger, "The Devaluation of Assets in Black Neighborhoods: The Case of Residential Property" (Brookings Institution, November 2018); see also Ta-Nehisi Coates, "The Case for Reparations," *The Atlantic*, June 2014; and Urban Institute, "Examining the Black Middle Class," September 2021.

143   **"Poor black people do not work"**: Coates, "The Case for Reparations."

144   **According to a study**: Chuck Collins, Dedrick Asante-Muhammad, Josh Hoxie, and Emanuel Nieves, *The Ever-Growing Gap: Without Change, African-American and Latino Families Won't Match White Wealth for Centuries* (Washington, DC: Institute for Policy Studies and Corporation for Enterprise Development, August 2016).

144   **What this estimate**: Ben Johnson, "The Great Horse Manure Crisis of 1894," Historic UK.

144   **Polling about interracial marriage**: Frank Newport, "In U.S., 87% Approve of Black-White Marriage, vs. 4% in 1958," Gallup, July 25, 2013.

145   **In earlier eras**: Steven Pinker, *The Better Angels of Our Nature: Why Violence Has Declined* (Penguin Books, 2012), 170.

146   **As the school's president**: Kathryn Vasel, "Georgetown to Offer Slave Descendants Preferential Admission Status," CNN, September 1, 2016.

147   **The bottom line**: C. Vann Woodward, *The Strange Career of Jim Crow* (New York: Oxford University Press, 1961), 49–51.

147   **Her ownership of a human**: Frederick Douglass, *Narrative of the Life of Frederick Douglass, an American Slave*, ed. John W. Blassingame, John R. McKivigan, and Peter P. Hinks, 5th ed. (New Haven, CT: Yale University Press, 2001), 32–36.

147   **"the death of the heart"**: James Baldwin, "A Conversation with James Baldwin," interview by Kenneth Clark, *The Negro and the American Promise*, May 1963, WGBH Education Foundation; available at the American Archive of Public Broadcasting.

147   **"whoever debases others"**: James Baldwin, *The Fire Next Time* (New York: Vintage International, 1992), 82.

147   **"future of the Negro"**: James Baldwin, *Conversations with James Baldwin*, ed. Fred L. Standley and Louis H. Pratt (Jackson: University Press of Mississippi, 1989), 82.

INDEX

Page numbers after 150 refer to endnotes.

and the remedying of past injustices, 12,
115–17, 124, 130
reparations, 19, 51, 103–4, 111–13,
138–39, 143–47

Kennedy, John F., 78, 98, 102
Kerner Commission (National Advisory
Commission on Civil Disorders),
2–3, 80, 82, 95
Keynesianism, 62, 64, 76, 86, 92, 99, 105
"King Cotton," 18–19, 21
King, Martin Luther, Jr., 77–79, 88–91,
95–96, 122, 136, 138
assassination of, 3, 90
birthday a national holiday, 117
on Black banking, 71–72
color-blindness of, 116
March on Washington, 74, 77, 107, 138
on violence, 85
Krippner, Greta, 93
Ku Klux Klan, 16, 22, 27, 32, 41–42, 45, 51
Kuhn, Clifford, 33

labor
class solidarity, 41, 55, 86
conflict and reform of capitalism, 38,
40–41
convict leasing, 19, 75
full employment, 94, 160
racial divisions in, 8
slavery, 1n, 2, 6, 9–10, 13–27, 72, 84–85,
114–16, 136, 139, 145–47
unions, 8, 38, 41–42, 43, 64, 86–87,
107–9, 118
wages, 15, 17, 64, 81, 118, 140
See also employment; unions
law enforcement
courts of law, 12, 17, 22–23, 62, 69, 116,
146
the criminalization of Blackness, 26, 45,
69, 87, 120–22, 128
the police state, 45, 87
political affordances of "tough on crime"
rhetoric, 121–22
public housing and incarceration, 122
War on Crime/War on Drugs, 87,
120–24

Levy, Jonathan, 76
Lew, Jack, 143
libertarians, 86, 105, 109, 112–13
Lincoln, Abraham, 15–16, 20, 26, 78
Lloyd's of London, 20
loans/lending. *See* credit/debt
Lochner v. New York (1905), 42
"lost cause narrative," 26
Ludlow Massacre of 1914, 43
lynchings, 12, 35, 36–37, 56, 62

MAGA realignment of the right, 6
Malcolm X, 6, 52, 72, 90–91
Mandate for Leadership book series, 121
March on Washington of 1941, 74
March on Washington of 1963, 74, 77,
107, 138
"market magic," 128–29
markets. *See* free-market capitalism
Marshall, Thurgood, 116
mass incarceration of Black men. *See* law
enforcement
McKnight, Gerald, 89
McLaurin, Dunbar S., 104
Memphis, TN, 3, 89
Michigan, 101
microcredit, 124–25
middle class (Black), 54, 56, 66, 69–70, 77,
110, 117–18, 143
middle class (white), 60–61, 65–69, 83, 86,
96, 117–18, 143
"military-industrial complex," 76, 94–96
Miller, Brad, 127
minimum wage (federal), 118
Minority Business Development Agency
grants, 119
Minority Enterprise Development Week,
119
"minority hiring" programs, 108
minority-owned businesses, 8, 105–8,
114–21
Mis-education of the Negro, The (Woodson),
57
"mismatch theory," 133
monetary policy, 5, 38–42, 60–64, 94,
100
monopolies, 38, 42, 43, 50, 63, 64

Norton Shorts

BRILLIANCE WITH BREVITY

W. W. Norton & Company has been independent since 1923, when William Warder Norton and Mary (Polly) D. Herter Norton first published lectures delivered at the People's Institute, the adult education division of New York City's Cooper Union. In the 1950s, Polly Norton transferred control of the company to its employees.

One hundred years after its founding, W. W. Norton & Company inaugurates a new century of visionary independent publishing with Norton Shorts. Written by leading-edge scholars, these eye-opening books deliver bold thinking and fresh perspectives in under two hundred pages.

Available Winter 2026

The Racial Wealth Gap: A Brief History by Mehrsa Baradaran

Imagination: A Manifesto by Ruha Benjamin

What's Real About Race? Untangling Science, Genetics, and Society by Rina Bliss

Offshore: Stealth Wealth and the New Colonialism by Brooke Harrington

Sex Beyond "Yes": Pleasure and Agency for Everyone by Quill R Kukla

Fewer Rules, Better People: The Case for Discretion by Barry Lam

Explorers: A New History by Matthew Lockwood

Wild Girls: How the Outdoors Shaped the Women Who Challenged a Nation by Tiya Miles

The Trafficker Next Door: How Household Employers Exploit Domestic Workers by Rhacel Salazar Parreñas

Gather: Black Food, Nourishment, and the Art of Togetherness by Ashanté M. Reese

The Moral Circle: Who Matters, What Matters, and Why by Jeff Sebo

Against Technoableism: Rethinking Who Needs Improvement by Ashley Shew

Fear Less: Poetry in Perilous Times by Tracy K. Smith

Literary Theory for Robots: How Computers Learned to Write by Dennis Yi Tenen

Forthcoming

Merlin Chowkwanyun on the social determinants of health

Daniel Aldana Cohen on eco-apartheid

Jim Downs on cultural healing

Reginald K. Ellis on Black education versus Black freedom

Nicole Eustace on settler colonialism

Agustín Fuentes on human nature

Justene Hill Edwards on the history of inequality in America

Destin Jenkins on a short history of debt

Kelly Lytle Hernández on the immigration regime in America

Natalia Molina on the myth of assimilation

Tony Perry on water in African American culture and history

Beth Piatote on living with history

Daniel Steinmetz-Jenkins on religion and populism

Onaje X. O. Woodbine on transcendence in sports